The Transformational Journey of a Young
Patient Undergoing Regression Therapy

Healing
Deep Hurt Within

Dr. Peter Mack

FOREWORD BY ANDY TOMLINSON

from the
heart press

Publication by From the Heart Press: First Publication September 2011
Website: www.fromtheheartpress.com

Text copyright: Peter Mack
ISBN: 978-0-9567887-1-9

A CIP catalogue record for this book is available from the British Library.

Design: Ashleigh Hanson, Email: hansonashleigh@hotmail.com

To contact Peter Mack email: dr02162h@yahoo.com.sg.

Contents

Disclaimer

This book is not intended to be a means to sensationalize hypnosis and regression therapy nor to promote them as a form of miracle cure. The author conforms to the view that hypnotherapy and regression therapy are complementary therapies and do not replace the practice of conventional medicine. Each patient's situation is unique and deserves individual attention. Likewise, those in the helping profession who are involved in assisting patients with traumatic experiences should consult the medical professionals if and when the need for medical attention arises.

Acknowledgments

Learning from experience is as old as the hills. We all learn valuable lessons from others who are able to show us their experience and connect their experience to our own. Towards this end I am exceedingly grateful to my patient, Petrina (pseudonym), for her courage and willingness to share the details of her healing experience with the readers. It is her desire that lessons learned from her transformational journey be shared as a source of inspiration for other patients in similar situations.

Only pseudonyms have been used for the characters appearing in this book. Furthermore, their personal characteristics have been modified or changed to protect their identities. I wish to express my thanks to the following people who have made this book a reality:

- Sister Susan Loh and Sister Tan Siok Bee for providing the needed nursing support and encouragement.
- The entire nursing team in G Clinic for their permission and cooperation to use the outpatient facility for the therapy.
- Dr. Vikram Jaisinghani and Dr. Darren Koh for reading an early draft of this book and providing constructive suggestions for revision.
- Dr. Ng Han Seong, Chairman of the Medical Board, and Ms. Tan-Huang Shuo Mei, Director of Communications, who gave permission for the use of the name of Singapore General Hospital as the contextual background of the story.
- Dr. Ong Biauw Chi and Ms. Serene Wong who provided ethical advice from the regulatory perspective of the Singapore Medical Council.
- Ms. Elizabeth Choo Mei Yue of SingHealth Legal Office who provided legal advice.

Foreword

I first met Peter back in 2009 when he was a student on a regression therapy training program that I was giving in Singapore. I never guessed then that this highly respected medical professional would become such a talented regression therapist and colleague, and go on to introduce regression therapy to the medical world in Singapore. Then he would collaborate on one of my books, *Transforming the Eternal Soul,* by writing a chapter on using regression therapy in a medical practice. So adding my comments to his first book on the subject is a delight for me.

Regression therapy and hypnosis have been used in all forms of psychotherapy over many years – either directly or indirectly. Simply by asking a client to focus inwardly they go into hypnotic trance. Or if a client is asked what was happening around the time they first had their problem, a simple regression takes place. Handling catharsis, frozen body memories from deep trauma, transformation, and integrating the experience into a client's current life require many more skills. Hypnosis has become widely accepted as a powerful tool in healing in many countries – as early as 1955 it was accepted by the British Medical Association as a valuable medical tool, and in 1958 by the American Medical Association. Regression therapy, which brings together hypnosis and regression techniques from other psychotherapies into one approach, has been slower in getting medical acceptance. This is perhaps because regression therapists, who respect their client's internal experiences, may work with what appear to be past lives or spiritual encounters. Culture or fear of working outside traditional boundaries may have contributed to this slow uptake. However, when medical professionals experience the rapid healing themselves or on their patients, views change.

To maintain standards I established an association for my regression therapy graduates called the *Spiritual Regression Therapy Association*, and working together with leading regression therapy schools a single international standard has been established through an organization called the *European Association of Regression Therapy*. This quickly expanded to work worldwide. Being one of the co-founders gave me the opportunity to contribute by being on the working group covering new training school acceptance. These associations draw on regression therapists from many backgrounds including psychotherapists and growing numbers of clinical psychologists, psychiatrists and medical doctors. All share the same realization of the power of this approach to healing.

This book is an absorbing account of one of Peter's patients. She was severely traumatized from emotionally crippling events over her life that left her feeling suicidal and abandoned. Unable to be healed by traditional medicine, this is a moving story of Peter's dedication to help her using hypnosis and regression therapy. Peter shares his concerns, insights and delight as the client is guided on her healing journey to full recovery. It's a testament of the single-minded determination Peter found while he was still busy as a full-time medical doctor in hospital. You will find it generates a roller coaster of emotions for the reader and is a great read.

Andy Tomlinson
Director for Training – Past Life Regression Academy
July 2011

Introduction

Hello darkness, my old friend,
I've come to talk with you again.
                                        – Paul Simon

Helping people in need brings joy to oneself. Realizing that the person you have helped is now able to help others is an even greater joy. This, in essence, is the motivation behind how this book has come to be written.

Decades back, there was little distinction between the concept of "healing", which belonged to the softer realm of emotions and spirituality, and "clinical treatment", which related to a more technical and controlled realm of medical expertise. However, as medical progress slanted towards science and technology, things became different. I grew up in a scientific environment and enjoyed abundant opportunities during my career in the application of medical science to correct human dysfunctions. After graduation, I was attracted to the specialty of surgery because the discipline provided me with the special skill of correcting pathological anatomy. For many years thereafter, the science of medicine captivated my interest. However, after three decades of clinical practice I looked back to re-examine the paradigm of disease causation, and I felt that something was missing. Each time I came face to face with patients presenting with medically unexplainable symptoms, the gap in our knowledge became more obvious.

The approach to unexplainable symptoms in conventional medicine has typically been to shroud the diagnostic problem under a terminological disguise. We tend to use clinical labels like "syndrome", "idiopathic" or "functional disorder" freely under such a circumstance. On the other hand we remain silent as to how much the use of such labels contributes to new knowledge or adds to our wisdom in helping our patients out of their distress.

The conventional medical paradigm teaches that all sicknesses fall into one of several physical processes such as inflammatory, genetic, vascular, degenerative, hormonal, infective, neoplastic or immunological. In contrast, emotional stress is traditionally considered as foreign to the list. At best it is relegated into the category of a trigger, but not an etiological factor. This is because the view of healing in modern medicine is a largely biological one. Few if any practitioners are prepared to explore the possibility of harnessing the power of thoughts, emotions and feelings to influence physical health.

Leveraging on emotions and thoughts for healing involves access to the unconscious mind. Milton Erickson, the father of modern hypnotherapy, once said that most of an individual's life is unconsciously determined. Yet, the unconscious is not necessarily unchangeable. The aim of psychodynamic psychotherapy is in fact to make the unconscious mind of the patient more conscious. We are aware that the positive value of psychotherapy is based on an individual's ability to change. Less often highlighted is the fact that this change is most effectively accomplished in the trance state when the patient focuses on his unconscious patterns, including his values and frames of reference.

To heal someone is to make the individual healthy, whole or sound. Although my own medical career has centered largely on the practice of surgery, I have over the years privately taken up studies in hypnotherapy. My personal interest in the unconscious has driven me to explore the restoration of health via a different realm.

The process of hypnosis allows direct access to the patient's unconscious mind. It has been noted that in many situations where conventional medicine has no solutions to offer, patients have been able to heal themselves by tapping into the power of their experience in the trance state. Trance is the state of the mind in which hypnosis takes place. It is an altered state of consciousness in which rapid learning and change are most likely to occur. I use the term synonymously with the hypnotic state in this book. The ability to get into trance is a valuable asset in healing. Under trance we can tap into the power of the unconscious mind to retrieve our forgotten learning, create changes and construct new behavioral patterns to restore health and become wholesome again.

Hypnosis has a tremendous potential to facilitate a variety of healing strategies. Its key effectiveness as a therapeutic modality depends in large measure on its capacity to excite the commitment and motivation of the patient. Simply entering the hypnotic state may induce relaxation and reduce stress, but it can in addition help to speed up the impact of psychotherapy.

This book is based on the true story of a young patient whose emotional trauma and psychological distress has been dealt with by hypnotic regression therapy in a hospital environment. The traditional medical model teaches us that patients who are unhappy, helpless and hopeless are at the grim endpoint of a mental disease process that requires pharmacotherapy. However, my studies in hypnosis have trained me to view depression differently. I prefer to see it as the beginning of an unfolding process of self-awareness. From such a perspective, afflicted patients can benefit from an integration of their psyche with their soma through the use of hypnosis. Furthermore their symptoms may be used as opportunities rather than catastrophes in the healing process. Replacing negative experiences with patterns that would benefit patients' mood, outlook and behavior is the ultimate goal in such a therapy.

Hypnotherapy encompasses a wide variety of methods and techniques that share a common concept. It is the concept that individuals often have more abilities than they may consciously realize. Regression is one specialized component that may be gainfully applied to patients with ongoing emotional difficulties resulting from negative past experiences. I have used regression therapy extensively on the patient in this book, and the positive clinical outcome and subsequent transformation comprise the bulk of the subject matter of this book.

Several lessons have been learned from this patient's transformational journey. In the first place, successful therapy requires close attention and often equates to a close personal attention to the patient. Secondly, depressive moods can be very constrictive. The feeling of sadness oppresses the mind, weighs down the body and darkens the spirit. Depressed patients may be fearful of emptiness because they get reminded of loneliness. When they experience life crises and emotional traumas, they need to understand that their recovery may be enhanced by their own active and creative involvement. Thirdly, an effective way of lifting a depressive mood involves the use of expressive therapy, be it in the form of writing or of drawing. Expressive therapy allows patients to activate or mobilize their own resources and facilitates the release of the creative spirit to evoke the core healing process.

Fourthly, I have learned that there is a right time for the therapist to tell a patient about his concerns and a right time to offer help. Obtaining the clinical history from an emotionally traumatized patient requires more patience and time than any other medical category of patients. In the process of elucidating the story of the life crisis during regression, the infusion of hope forms a very important part of the therapy. One must learn to talk more when patients are on track and observe silence when they are upset. Making a record of the observations of response and regularly analyzing them is fundamental to a dynamic therapy. In short, learning and healing are inseparable in the therapy process.

Fifthly, forgiveness short-circuits grief, brings inner peace and restores physical health. It requires letting go and is a

4

powerful alkali that neutralizes the acidity of anger, hate and bitterness. The forces of forgiving are latent and they operate during a crisis when we find unsuspected strength within us. Sometimes a spontaneous transformation may take place in us. In many ways the act of forgiving is the key to healing the hurt that lies within.

Lastly, in learning to give therapy, we ought to value times of darkness as much as periods of enlightenment. We use patients' obstacles to growth instead of promising their complete disappearance. In times of darkness the creativity allowed by the confusion is the prerequisite to obtaining clarity of solution to the problem.

This book has been written with three types of reader in mind: first, the therapist, who may find the story resonating with his own clinical experience, second, the medical practitioner, who is keen to understand how alternative therapies may possibly complement modern medicine, and third, the patient, who is on the desperate lookout for alternative treatment options when pharmacotherapy alone has proven inadequate in his or her situation.

Chapter One

Dire Need

*The act of compassion begins with full attention, just as rapport
does. You have to really see the person. If you see the person,
then naturally, empathy arises. If you tune into the other person,
you feel with them. If empathy arises and if that person is in dire
need, then empathic concern can come. You want to help them,
and then that begins a compassionate act.*

– Daniel Goleman

The telephone rang. It was mid-morning of Wednesday,
24 November 2010, and I was in the specialist outpatient
department running my morning clinic. I picked up the
receiver and heard Nurse Beatrice's voice on the other
end of the line.

"Good morning, Dr. Mack," she began, in her usual
phlegmatic tone. "We have a patient in the Neurology Ward
needing your help."

Beatrice herself was an Advanced Practice Nurse attached to
the discipline of Neurology. A dynamic and forward-looking
nurse, she had been very busy lately because she was in her last
months of completing her postgraduate nursing studies. It so
happened that she and I had been fellow enthusiasts in the
practice of hypnotherapy over the past two years. However,
because of her recent commitment to her studies, she had lately
been requesting assistance from me for some of her patients. So
this call did not come as a surprise.

"She is in fact a staff member of the Ophthalmology
Department," she began. "She fainted at work and has very deep

emotional issues arising from out of her relationship and career problems. She used to be a star performer at work, but is now facing problems with her work supervisor. She is so weakened emotionally that I think we ought to help her. The ward doctors have done their morning round and are discharging her today. I think she needs a month of hospitalization leave to rest at home and get treated in the meanwhile. I have suggested that to the intern, and have also told the patient that she must see you soon after her discharge. How can I arrange that?"

This was Beatrice's usual style of communication. She has a way of persuading people to do things and move into uncharted territories. The clinical problem as described over the phone did not sound like the usual type of patient that Beatrice would normally refer to me for hypnotherapy. There was a subtle anxiety in her voice, and an unmistakable sense of concern over the patient's well-being. This was not surprising. Of late Beatrice had a reputation of being a Miss-fix-it for all social and emotional problems in the Neurology Department.

I have never turned down a request from Beatrice. As I was still busy with my morning clinic, I told her to pass my mobile phone number to the patient and that I would pay a visit to the patient in the ward later on.

By late morning, after completing my last patient consultation, I began walking towards the inpatient block of the hospital. Being in a contemplative mood, my intuitive self was telling me that I was about to come face to face with a major challenge. As I entered the doorway of the Neurology Ward a senior male nurse greeted me politely.

"Sir, are you Dr. Mack?

"Yes." I nodded. "I have come to see a patient who has been referred by Nurse Beatrice."

"Oh, I am afraid she has just gone for her EEG. Would you like to see her in the EEG room instead? It is just down the corridor."

"No worry. I'll come back later." I gave a smile.

"Sure. She is a young girl and is in bed 25/7."

A young girl … hmmm … I was intrigued! I honestly was expecting to face a middle-aged woman in the midst of a midlife crisis!

An hour later, I returned to the ward and came face to face with the patient for the first time. Her name was Petrina. She was a very sweet-looking lady with long, dark hair, brown eyes, and a sharp chin with dimples on both sides of her cheek. She was 25 years of age and her face had the shape of a melon seed. She was attired in turquoise hospital pajamas and seated on her bed, quietly sobbing away.

As I came closer, I immediately noted her frailness and undernourishment. Her body weight was in fact only 35 kilograms at that point in time. Her hair was mid-arm in length, with a scalp parting to the left of the midline causing her slanting hairdo to cover her right forehead and the lateral half of her right eye. Behind the scattered hair strands, I discerned teardrops rolling down both her cheeks. She was in a daze, and seemed to be overwhelmed by sorrow. It was very obvious that she was going through an emotional crisis.

I introduced myself and noticed that she barely had the stamina to shake my hand. Through the mistiness in her eyes I could sense her emotions of agony as she struggled to start a dialogue with me. My heart suddenly felt heavy.

I pulled a chair and sat down by her bedside. She spoke softly but very intelligently. She worked as a patient service counter clerk in the Ophthalmology Department and had a blackout at her Director's office the day before. After the hospital's Code Blue team had attended she was brought to the Emergency Room and subsequently admitted to the Neurology Ward for further investigation. She acknowledged that Nurse Beatrice had talked to her at length earlier about treatment options and given her my contact number.

As I listened, I noticed that she looked pale, fatigued and downtrodden. Submerged under her quiet complexion was a desperate cry for help. She began talking about her clinical issues but to my horror, her memory recall was poor and her story disjointed. Furthermore, her narrative was punctuated by sobs in between. Making sense of her clinical problem was a challenge.

From what I could gather, she came from a Buddhist background. She had a very unhappy marriage, had been through three abortions and had to work hard to pay off her husband's mounting debts. She had been suffering from throbbing headaches since, gone into depression and started to lose her memory. Since then she had been experiencing blackouts. She recalled that her fainting attacks started as early as January 2010. These attacks were always sudden, unpredictable and usually preceded by a sudden ringing sound in the ears, light-headedness and a feeling of nausea. She had appeared at the Emergency Room on multiple occasions for her fainting spells and there were no signs of her getting better.

In order to obtain a better chronology of her illness, I accessed the hospital's computer records system. Petrina was first seen in the Emergency Dept in Singapore General Hospital (SGH) in October 2010. She was noted to have a syncopal attack after lunch and was referred by the Staff Clinic to the Emergency Department. She felt giddy, experienced tinnitus and subsequently blacked out. Fortunately she was caught by one of her colleagues in time and prevented from falling. At that time she was at the tail end of her menstrual period. Since the CT scan of the head was normal, she rejected the idea of being hospitalized for further investigation.

She fainted again on 4th November and experienced difficulty in breathing at that time. She was seen in the Emergency Room in Changi General Hospital (CGH). Apparently she had a bout of upper respiratory infection during the preceding week and again was not keen for hospital admission. While queuing up to make payment at the billing counter she suffered another blackout. She eventually changed her mind and was admitted as an inpatient during that visit. After an overnight observation in CGH, she was discharged the following day with the presumptive diagnosis of a flu-induced syncope.

Just prior to this admission, she blacked out while at work during a busy clinic hour. Seconds before she collapsed, she recalled a masculine voice speaking to her: "Hey, Petrina, you are too tired, it's time for you to get a good sleep and don't wake up." She fainted immediately after that, resulting in a commotion at the workplace. After being brought to the Emergency Room her heart rate was noted to be very fast, at 173 per minute. At the same time she was experiencing "pressing" chest pain. Not feeling comfortable with her syncope, the doctor at the Emergency Room decided to admit her to the Neurology Ward for further investigation.

During the ward round that morning, the team of Neurology doctors decided that she was well enough to go home and return to work. This seemed to have irritated Sister Louise, who was the Nursing Officer in charge of the ward.

Apparently Sister Louise had spotted Petrina's deep-seated emotions earlier during her nursing round. She alerted the intern, Dr. Shanti, that Petrina would need special attention for her emotional issues and pointed out that her clinical problem was neither neurological nor psychiatric in nature. Rather she perceived her as a deeply traumatized patient who needed a long period of medical leave to recover. Dr. Shanti did not feel comfortable with her suggestion however. After all, the patient did not exhibit any signs of physical, laboratory or radiological abnormalities to warrant a long leave. In the absence of a formal recommendation from a more senior doctor from a relevant specialty, she felt that it was too much of a responsibility for her to grant a lengthy medical leave.

Sister Louise had many years of neurosurgical nursing experience in another hospital before being posted to SGH, and was not someone who would give in so easily. She understood from her past clinical experience, that many patients fainting from vasovagal responses had underlying emotional problems, and Petrina fitted into that category. If none of the ward doctors were prepared to offer help she would not hesitate to call upon external assistance on her own. Nurse Beatrice promptly came along at her request, and spoke to Petrina. However, as she was already scheduled to go on study leave soon, she was not available to take on the longer-term commitment of looking after Petrina.

In the midst of my interaction with Petrina, she suddenly interrupted. "Oh, sorry! My brother is here to visit me." A young man neatly dressed and wearing a corporate name tag was standing behind me.

The lunch-time visitors' hour had just begun. Petrina's brother worked as an executive in the Human Resource Department. His office was in close proximity and he had taken advantage of the physical convenience to pay his sister a visit. I politely excused myself and reassured Petrina that I would resume my conversation with her later in the afternoon.

I returned to the Neurology Ward at 3:30 pm. To my surprise, Petrina had regained her composure and her complexion was very different. She had tidied her hair, dried her eyes, and powdered her face. This time she greeted me gracefully with a smile and appeared more aware of her surroundings. She was able to deliver a more coherent story this time.

Petrina went through three abortions in 2006, 2009 and 2010. She terminated her first pregnancy in 2006 just before her marriage. At that time she and Joshua, her spouse-to-be, decided that they were neither financially nor socially ready to look after a child. Soon after their marriage she realized that her husband was not the responsible individual she had hoped for. The symptom of throbbing sensation in her head started as she was facing the

12

problems of a family start-up. She also noticed that the symptom would worsen each time she listened to music.

In 2007 her marriage soured. Joshua worked as operation manager in a jewelry firm, and a year into the marriage he expressed his desire to further his studies. He wanted to study for a Diploma in Business Management and needed money. Petrina on the other hand was working in a beauty salon. She was a confident individual and a high-flier and soon became the manager of a department within the beauty business. However, she had to work very hard every day of the week, doing sales and managing the call center. On top of her base pay of $2100 her commission could be substantial and sometimes top up her monthly income to as much as $5000. However, she had to fund her husband's studies and pay all his extravagant bills. Depression set in as her finances became tight. Her insomnia started to become increasingly problematic. She was a light sleeper to start with and the sleep deprivation of the past three years had taken a toll on her. As a result she felt increasingly tired in the mornings.

I was watching her facial expression as I listened to the story intently. Behind her mask of elegance, I could sense a mix of sorrow and pain breaking through as she talked.

In 2009 she had her second abortion and became acutely depressed after that. "I can hear a child speaking to me: Where is my Mum?" she said with a sob.

"Is it a real voice that you actually hear" I asked with curiosity.

"Yes, it is a voice, but its frequency of appearance has diminished after taking medication," she replied.

She dared not tell her family members, especially her mother, about the abortion. Her mother had also been a victim of depression for the past twenty years, and her problem arose out of her own marriage failure. Apparently her mother had divorced and remarried. Her father on the other hand was now living with one of her maternal aunts (Fig. 1).

Fig. 1: Genogram – Depression in the family

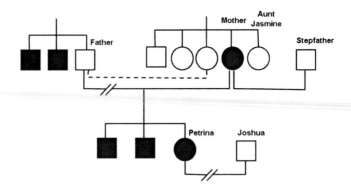

With her deteriorating health Petrina soon found herself unable to continue with her hectic job in the beauty salon. She resigned and decided to join the healthcare sector as a patient services counter clerk for a salary of only $1300 per month.

In the meanwhile, the guilt from her abortions was consuming her. By January 2010 she began to develop fainting spells. Initially she would experience a ringing sound as a prodromal symptom, followed immediately by a blackout that could last anything from a few minutes to half an hour. Each episode was accompanied by cold sweat. These fainting episodes became more frequent and by May 2010 they occurred as often as twice to three times a week. The duration of the blackouts also increased. At one stage she fainted and remained unconscious for eight hours before waking up.

These blackouts had made her very tired physically and mentally. Six months ago, she reached a stage where she requested unpaid leave to rest, but her supervisor had flatly refused her. She then forced herself to continue working until she was about to shut down physically. Her memory of people around her, including some of her colleagues and friends, were being lost. At this time, she recalled a "psychologist" friend of hers by the name of Aaron who was helping her out through this very difficult period. However, for some reason, her memory of him had also faded.

Petrina had picked up a smoking habit over the past three years. She had been the one purchasing cigarettes for her husband, and after a while she joined him and they started smoking together. In her working life she could smoke as much as 20 to 30 cigarettes per day, but fortunately she had not become psychologically dependent on it as yet.

In August 2010 she discovered that her husband had an affair with her good friend Hazel, but again she had lost most of the memory regarding the identity of Hazel and the social group to which she and Hazel both belonged.

"Somehow I do not want to remember them. I do not want to share what I remember on that day. The name of the woman is Hazel. I get agitated with that name," she remarked with a spark of anger in her eyes. "She was migrating to Canada. I was helping her to pack her stuff to move house," she recalled, "and then I saw a photo of her and my husband together beneath her bed." Tears were welling up in her eyes. "The whole group of friends was aware of the affair but did not tell me," she continued bitterly. "I gave up the entire group of friends ever since," she sobbed.

Petrina had already filed for divorce. However, her mother-in-law was 80 years old and had treated her very well. Unfortunately the old lady still had to work as a dish-washer in a restaurant to supplement the income at home. With the divorce, her husband had to sell off the house to pay off his own debts. After that her mother-in-law would have no place to stay, and this seemed to have aggravated Petrina's sense of guilt. Ever since the divorce, Petrina had shifted out and was staying with her mother.

On 10th November, a week after her discharge from CGH, Petrina consulted her family doctor in Old Airport Road, Dr. Wong, for her problems. After diagnosing her anxiety state he prescribed Nordazepam and Alprazolam for her. He had earlier treated her successfully for her throbbing headaches and had advised her that her symptoms of syncope and insomnia originated from her unconscious mind. Both the drugs he prescribed belonged to the minor tranquillizer class. Nordazepam had anxiolytic and sedative properties, and Petrina had cautiously consumed only three tablets to date. Alprazolam, on the other hand, was a short-acting drug and was used as adjunctive treatment for anxiety with moderate depression. She was reluctant to take it and I noticed the medication packet had been unopened so far.

Petrina's general health had been rapidly deteriorating since the onset of her anxiety and depression. Her family doctor had arranged for her an appointment to see a psychiatrist in Gleneagles Hospital in January 2011, but she was not keen. She did not want to get herself stigmatized as a mental patient, nor could she afford the private medical specialist fees. I later realized that her husband had taken all her money since she initiated the divorce. He had also, without warning, withdrawn the last $7000 from her bank account that was held in joint name with him.

I was disturbed by Petrina's sense of desperation. Yet at her young age, I felt she could make good use of the remarkable capacity within herself to recover from the hurt she had experienced. Perhaps she could perceive her depression as a wake-up call? Maybe she would be able to see her present condition as the start of a bigger journey? However, her wholeness of mind and integrity of self had somehow slipped away and she needed help to find them again. Was I the appropriate person to help her? Would she believe that this bigger journey could eventually lead her to becoming whole and happy again? I knew very well that if I were to commit, it would also be an opportunity for a deep change in myself. After some thought, I reassured Petrina that I would help her all the way.

The next issue concerned her medical leave. I walked over to the central nurses' station, retrieved her case file, sat down and wrote a page-long memo to Dr. Shanti, stating all the reasons why I backed the decision for Petrina to have a month of medical leave.

After work that evening, I mentally reviewed the story that had been given to me. There were many gaps. I could understand the reason for Petrina to repress her memory of those friends who had "betrayed" her, but why did she also forget those of her work colleagues and her psychologist friend who bothered to help her? Also, if the second abortion had been a major source of her emotional trauma, why did she go through the trauma of a third pregnancy and abortion. On a more pragmatic level, I wondered if her fading memory would allow her to remember me as her therapist, when I next met her …?

I decided that, at this stage, I needed to probe further while waiting for more information.

Chapter Two
Getting Stuck

Desperation is the raw material of drastic change. Only those who can leave behind everything they have ever believed in can hope to escape.

– William S. Burroughs

After my morning ward round the next day, I dropped by the Neurology Ward to look for Petrina. A staff nurse met me on the corridor and promptly informed me that she had been discharged the previous evening with the diagnosis of a vasovagal syncope. The findings of the EEG, CT brain and the stand-up/tilt test were normal. The results of the sympathetic skin response test were in keeping with the understanding that her repeated attacks of vasovagal syncope had come from pooling of blood in the limbs that caused reduced blood flow to the brain. What was comforting to hear was that Dr. Shanti had eventually issued her one month of hospitalization leave and it was on the basis of my recommendation.

Petrina was resting at home when I called her. She did not sound as if she had problems remembering who I was or recalling the content of our conversation yesterday. After an evening's rest she had come to terms with how to manage her blackouts. She had decided that her syncope was so unpredictable and menacing that it was no longer safe for her to leave the house alone. Instead, she preferred to arrange for a family member to accompany her to hospital for the next appointment. On that note I offered to see her the following Monday afternoon in the hospital outpatient clinic.

Petrina's problem was off my mind for the rest of the day. However, the following evening I received an anxious email from her. Apparently she had chosen to follow her mother out of the house to visit their doctor for a scheduled appointment during the late Friday afternoon. Her brother was driving and while inside the car, sitting next to her mum, she experienced a sudden blackout.

"I had a blackout again last night on the way to my mum's doctor's appointment in the car. After that for about 30 minutes, all of a sudden I couldn't recall where I was and what's the purpose of coming to the doctor with my mum. Shortly after another 20 minutes I started to recall back. Seems like I'm getting worse. I'm starting to worry I might start to forget everything eventually ..."

There was a clear depressing tone in her message. I pondered over her problem. She had been suffering from traumatic memories and her emotionally charged experiences had led to the development of signs and symptoms of dissociative amnesia. Her repeated memory blackouts seemed like a manifestation of a denial response to me. I had not been too comfortable in sinking myself into this difficult clinical problem of hers, but I believed I had the tools to uncover the root of her emotional trigger.

I called Petrina up to reassure her. Healing in her situation must begin with hope. She must know that she could make a difference to herself in how she would feel and how she would live her life. Recalling that she was of Buddhist faith, I asked about her prior experience with meditation. She had none. I persuaded her to learn and get started on the grounds that meditation was proven to be valuable for decreasing stress and quieting the mind.

Some time ago, I watched and listened to a couple of really soothing meditation videos on Youtube. One of them, titled

"Guided Meditation – Deep Relaxation$^©$" showed a clip of ocean waves lapping the shore against the backdrop of a setting sun. In addition there was a guided meditation script with a background of calming music. Then I remembered also identifying a second video clip called "Ultra Deep Guided Meditation for You" that contained hypnotic animation graphics in addition to its sound effects.

I forwarded both links to Petrina. She promised me that she would make good use of them. Little did I realize at this stage that she had embarked on learning one of the most useful self-management tools of her life.

****

Over the weekend, Nurse Beatrice had left for Australia for her clinical attachment. I updated her on Petrina's progress and, in particular, described to her about the fainting spells. Interestingly, she had a very different perspective of the syncope and was of the opinion that implicit suggestions might play a big part in her case. She wrote about her initial conversation and experience with her:

"Thanks for the update. By the way, let me share with you that Petrina saw a general practitioner who told her: '*I saw exactly the same case as you, and she is now not able to wake up from her sleep, dazed ...*' Talking about the power of suggestion, it's happening to her. Petrina herself mentioned that she knows there is nothing wrong with her. I also told her usually all the tests will be normal and she will need some kind of therapy."

I mulled over Beatrice's words and chuckled to myself. Well, if Petrina had such a high level of suggestibility, she would be an ideal candidate for hypnotherapy and a blessing.

****

On the Monday afternoon Petrina turned up to my clinic for her first therapy session. Her brother had driven her to SGH from her home at Tampines and she had taken advantage of the time in the car while stuck in a traffic jam to listen to the music and meditation script of the two videos that she had managed to download onto her iPhone.

She appeared in a plain blouse with a dark skirt. She had powdered her face and enhanced her appearance with glued-on eyelashes. She was visibly struggling with a weary countenance and beneath her tired exterior was a partially submerged sense of anguish. There was a set of beautiful artwork on her manicured nails on her fingers and toes. It was an attractive crimson-colored design that had taken her three hours to create. I learned later from her that nail art had always been her interest and she had wanted to take up a Course Diploma as a nail technician at one stage. Although it was a very tiring hobby, she enjoyed it because the process of creating the nail art made her "feel confident and in control".

I had a very brief conversation with her eldest brother who accompanied her to the clinic. He surprised me with a casual remark that he had not been in contact with his sister Petrina for the past three years and had no clue why and how she had suddenly become so ill! It struck me that Petrina had been hiding her predicament from not only her mother, but her siblings as well. Subsequently she told me the reason for her silence was because had her brother known the things Joshua had done to her, he would have beaten her ex-husband up. She did not want her brother to end up in the police station.

Inside the consultation room, Petrina opened up an envelope with a formal referral letter from Dr. Shanti of Neurology. A detailed clinical summary was enclosed. As I browsed through the document, a piece of detail caught my attention. There was an entry in the clinical notes that Petrina had her first syncopal attack as a child. I asked her and she confirmed it, adding that the attack occurred around the time when her mother was preparing for a divorce from her father.

Since her discharge from the Neurology Ward five days ago, she had not been sleeping well and her blackouts and memory loss continued to be a source of worry. On the other hand her family members were already getting used to her frequent syncope. With the attacks, her moods would fluctuate and be dominated by specific emotions from time to time. What was remarkable was that she was able, as a patient, to choose very apt descriptors for her symptoms.

She had been experiencing feelings of "being pressed" whenever she tried to recall her past. "It is like being locked in or trapped in a room and unable to get out," she described. "It is like a feeling of being encaged."

I listened carefully and took note of her precise description. In my role as a therapist, I was on the lookout for feelings and emotions that could potentially be useful as affect bridges for regression therapy.

She updated her family doctor, Dr. Wong, about her uncertainty of consulting a private psychiatrist compared to receiving hypnotherapy from a public hospital. To her surprise Dr. Wong advised her to stick to my appointment today and said that he was confident that hypnotherapy could be a better option.

A few colleagues had called her at home over the weekend but the worrisome part was that she could not recall their exact identities. I took the opportunity to begin the session by explaining to her that hypnotherapy was a powerful tool in helping patients to recall forgotten events.

"Hypnosis is but a state of focused concentration," I emphasized. "We go in and out of hypnotic states all the time and shift our focus of attention from within to without." I quoted a few examples that included watching television and driving on a highway. I explained how in a trance state one's conscious awareness could be suspended while the mind focused on inner thoughts and feelings. Also, during trance she would be able to gain access to memories not readily available in the waking state, particularly her repressed personal memories.

I spent the next several minutes in providing her with information on what to expect in her first hypnosis session and the nature of the verbal suggestions I would be giving. I explained how in her body's relaxed state, her mind's memory would begin to sharpen. I cited examples of my previous success in regressing patients back to their childhood to help them elicit memories of their forgotten traumas and help them get over those painful experiences.

Next, the nurse chaperone helped her to the couch. Then I turned on some relaxing music in the room and allowed a couple of minutes for her to settle down. We were ready to begin.

With her eyes closed, I asked her to take three deep breaths slowly and focus her feeling on the movement of the air flowing in and out of her chest. With each inhalation I suggested to her that she was breathing in relaxation and with each exhalation she was letting out pent-up tension from her body. After a couple of minutes, she settled down into a quiet calmness.

Next I guided her on a process of progressive relaxation of her different groups of body muscles. I began with suggestions on how she could actively relax the muscles on the top of her scalp and gradually moved the relaxation down to her forehead, face, jaw, neck, shoulders, arms and forearms, back muscles and her chest. I noticed that her eyelids began to flicker, and that gave me the indication that she was deepening in her hypnotic state. I continued with her relaxation process to her abdominal wall muscles, pelvis, hips, thighs, calves, ankles and down to the soles, at the end of which she was completely relaxed. This slow induction process seemed to have worked very well for her.

Next I employed the staircase imagery and guided her mind's eye to visualize herself standing on top of a staircase. Then, as I counted slowly backwards from ten to one, she deepened her trance effectively as she visualized herself stepping down the stairs with each successive count. To verify her trance depth, I tested for both eyelid and arm catalepsy and she passed both tests.

After about twenty minutes of relaxation and deepening, I was satisfied that she had good hypnotizability. Then I gradually emerged her out of her trance by counting backwards from five to one. As I reached the count of one, she lifted her eyelids slowly, looking a little dazed.

"How did it go?" I asked gently.

"Relaxed," she whispered, still staring dreamily at the ceiling above her.

Without further ado I immediately asked her to close her eyes again and rapidly brought her down into a trance state once more. I had chosen to take advantage of the fractionation effect. This was because with hypnotic processes, a patient entering the hypnotic state a second time shortly after the first tends to quickly reach a hypnotic state deeper than before. I next put my right palm gently over her forehead and said in a low tone, "Go deep." Within seconds she was in a deep trance, and ready for the next phase of therapy.

Chapter Three

Feeling Trapped

People are trapped in history and history is trapped in them.
— *James Arthur Baldwin*

P etrina was still on the couch and in the midst of a deep trance state. I realized that Nurse Beatrice's assessment of her hypnotizability was accurate. She was indeed a highly suggestible subject. Without further ado, I decided to go ahead with the regression therapy.

A regression is a process in which a hypnotized patient recalls a series of memories from the unconscious mind under the guide of the therapist. Gaining access to the patient's emotions is far easier under trance. Also, the individual's awareness is enhanced and the memory tends to be more vivid.

One of the gemstones I learned in my hypnotherapy training is that the best results in therapy always come from identifying the initial offending event of a distressing symptom. By getting the patient to relearn and reframe the past experience under trance the symptom could be released and healing accomplished. Regression is the appropriate technique to be used for this purpose. Without releasing the root cause, the unconscious mind is capable of returning to the same problem at a later time.

Petrina's most recent feeling of "being locked in a room and unable to get out" sounded to me like a good starting point for the therapy. The phrase seemed to contain a strong emotional component. My intention was to get her unconscious mind connected with a past incident in which she was sensitized to that trapped emotion.

"I want you now to focus your conscious awareness on your feelings of being pressed, being trapped or being enclosed," I began, "… and keep focusing on it."

She remained still and motionless. I made her repeat the phrase "I am trapped" verbally a few times and waited. She stayed quiet. Then I followed up with a technique to enhance her awareness of the emotion.

"As you continue to focus on the emotion of being trapped or locked, I am going to count from one to ten to amplify the intensity of those emotions. One, two … your emotions are building up … three, four, five … your emotions are getting stronger and stronger … six, seven … your emotions are getting more intense … eight, nine … getting very strong now … and ten … your emotional intensity is at its maximum now."

I noticed a slight muscle twitch on her face, as if a deeper process was at work. Then I continued.

"Now, as I count backwards from ten to one you will go back to a past event that is connected with these emotions. Ten, nine, eight, seven, six, five, four, three, two and … one."

Something significant was happening. Petrina started to talk the moment I reached the count of one.

"Bleeding …" she said softly. I was a little startled as her eyes were gradually welling up with tears. The affect bridge had successfully connected Petrina with a painful experience of the past.

"Where are you now?" I asked.

"At the bottom of the stairs … bleeding away."

"What happened to you?"

"I'm pregnant. My husband has pushed me down the stairs," she said with a sob.

"How do you describe your emotions right now?"

"I hate him … why did he do that to me?" Tears were welling up rapidly in her eyes.

She was visibly upset. I waited as her emotions were quickly building up. Then she burst out crying and was in full catharsis. It took some time before she could completely release a major installment of trapped emotions. After a few minutes she began to quieten down.

"Take a deep breath … and tell me what happened."

"I am tired," she said, after resuming her voice. "I have to work, do the laundry and cook for him. I never ask him where he goes, and what he does. Why … all the bills? He's working and I'm working and I am the one making the payment. Money is never enough. I do not want to ask him for help or we get into a quarrel."

There was a pause.

"He walked away with Hazel." I recalled Hazel as the name of her best friend with whom her husband had an affair. "I called my friend to send me to a GP. The GP gave me some medicine to stop my bleeding. He (Joshua) did not want the baby. I went to the gynecology clinic alone and did the abortion … The abortion is over. I miss my baby."

"What happened next?"

"I am at home now, waiting for him. He never came back."

"What is your emotion like at this stage?"

"Hate … I hate him for betraying me." She started crying again.

"What are your thoughts that go with the hatred?"

"How can my good friend (Hazel) be doing this to me?" she said bitterly with tears rolling down her cheeks again.

I waited. Several moments passed before the heat of her emotions went past its crescendo. Then she continued talking.

"I am now looking at all the bills. I have to sell everything off to pay his debts."

"What are your emotions then?"

"I feel trapped …" she said in a desperate tone.

Bingo! This was the same phrase that had been used as the affect bridge and it was clear that she had regressed back to a sensitizing event. I had learned from my earlier training that locating the initial sensitizing event was crucial in therapy. What she just described seemed like the core life event that had produced her perception of being "trapped" in a desperate situation.

"Why is it that I have to take on everything and make all the payments?" she continued. "I went back home to my mother. Mum tells me to talk to him. He never came back. I waited for his call ... Not one ... not even a message. I don't know what to do ... Then he called and asked me for money again. I did not give it to him. He beat me up. Then he went to the bank and transferred all the money out from the account. I'm left with nothing ..."

"How did you feel at this stage?"

"Lost."

"What happened next?"

"Aaron helped me –" She suddenly stopped. I noted a slight jerk of her head, following which she snapped out of hypnosis.

Petrina opened her eyes wide, looking half dazed. She had come out of trance abruptly and by herself. I was not quite sure why this happened when the session had gone smoothly so far. I did notice, however, this happened at the mention of the name Aaron, the psychologist friend who supposedly had helped her. Little did I suspect that this snapping out of trance was to become a recurrent phenomenon that would cause major disruption to her subsequent therapy sessions.

Without much ado, I instructed Petrina to close her eyes again while she was still in a semi-dreamy state. I brought her down into a hypnotic state once more.

"Relax yourself as you focus on the feeling of being trapped and being locked in ... and as you do so, let the images form in your mind ... Now tell me where you are and what is happening."

"I am at home with my mum and dad," she whispered.

"How old are you now?" I asked.

"Seven," she replied.

She had spontaneously jumped to a much earlier event in her life and I decided to work with whatever might emerge.

"What is happening now?"

"Dad is beating up Mum. He uses a belt … Mum locked herself up in a room."

Again, bingo! Petrina's feeling of "being locked in" seemed self-explanatory now.

"What happened next?"

"Dad took all the money and went to gamble."

"How did you feel?"

"I was scared. There was nothing I could do," she said in a desperate tone.

"What happened next?"

"Dad was gambling at home with his friends. I was hungry and asked for food. He used a cigarette to burn my face and told my mum that it was an accident. My head was painful from the burn. We had no money to see the doctor." Her voice was tremulous.

Pain was discernible in her voice. It seemed like I had trampled on an Inner Child problem. I also began to understand the emotional foundation as to why Petrina started to develop fainting spells during her primary school age. She later told me that her father was so addicted to gambling that he would wait for her mother to come home on pay day. Then, together with her aunt, the two of them would drag her to the automated teller machine to withdraw her entire salary for the month. Then they would run away with the money to gamble.

To cope with the situation, her mother had learned to stay late in her office on pay day, withdraw the money and use it to purchase food, especially canned food, before returning home. Despite this, there were still instances where her father would go to the extent of removing some of the canned food from home to convert them into cash for gambling.

My mind worked quickly to decide on the next step of the therapy. The abandoned Inner Child inside Petrina was obviously crying out for help through the vehicle of her current illness. With the lack of nurturance of her Inner Child, I decided to switch technique to let her discover her own "inner parent" within her unconscious.

I deepened her trance state and said: "Come back to the present age and see yourself as an adult ... Now bring your adult self to meet the young Petrina again ... Do you see her there?"

"Yes."

"What would your adult self say to comfort the young Petrina?"

"It will soon be over," she said with a soothing tone.

"What did the younger Petrina say in response?"

"I am suffering. What should I do?" There was a sound of sorrow in the voice.

"How did the older self respond to that?"

"You have no one to rely on except yourself. You will be free." This was uttered in a mature tone.

I gave Petrina a soft pillow, and said gently, "Go nearer to the young Petrina. Maybe you would like to tell her she is a good girl and give her a hug for a few moments."

After the Inner Child integration process was completed, I brought Petrina to a place of healing. Using guided imagery, I brought her to the front of a still pond and allowed her to imagine a pebble being thrown into the pond sending out ripples of relaxation to the periphery of the pool. I asked her to imagine that each word I uttered would be like a pebble tossed into the still water. She stayed calm and relaxed.

Following that I asked her to visualize standing beneath a waterfall and feel the warm water flowing gently down the top of her head, and all the way down the body, cleansing her of all tension.

By now two and a half hours had passed. Petrina emerged from the hypnotic state looking visibly tired. We both felt that it had been a fruitful session.

She dried her tears and finished a cup of hot Milo before leaving the consultation room. I reminded her that her therapy sessions would necessarily be intensive from now onwards. She understood and agreed to return for follow-up treatment the next day.

Petrina excused herself to go to the washroom and I took the opportunity to enjoy a short break. Moments later, a clinic nurse brought to my attention that Petrina, on her way out had a near blackout in the washroom. She managed to support herself in time and she narrowly escaped a fall.

This was unexpected on my part. The therapy had gone smoothly and I had no reason to expect her clinical symptoms to return so soon. I brought her back to the consultation room to rest on a chair. Five minutes later, after she had stabilized, I decided to accompany her to the passenger pickup point of the hospital entrance. She telephoned her brother, who then drove from home to pick her up from the hospital. Although she had been through a long and tiring therapy session, she put on a smile before she departed in the car.

****

That evening, after work, I left the hospital in a relaxed mood to attend a dinner appointment with two friends. However, in the midst of my dinner, Petrina called.

Apparently, soon after she arrived home, she began to develop a headache. The moment she closed her eyes she began to hear voices. Among the voices she could recognize a quarrel between her ex-husband Joshua and Hazel. By the time she called me, she could not recall the content of the conversation between the voices. She felt frustrated and worried.

It sounded like a flashback and I did not want her to be alarmed. I reassured her that she was going through an expected reaction immediately following an intensive therapy session.

Later that evening, I mused over the background history of childhood abuse. In my previous studies I learned about how women who had been involved with abusive people could unconsciously attempt to rewrite their past. Sigmund Freud called this tendency to re-enact the past as "repetition-compulsion" which may translate into an unconscious tendency for one to be attracted to the same type of abusive people over and over again in one's life. Was it because Petrina had missed her father's love that she subsequently became involved with a spouse who was very much like her father? And she was trying to make him love her?

Chapter Four
Surrendering to Change

If we openly declare what is wrong with us, what is our deepest need, then perhaps the death and despair will by degrees disappear.

– *J.B. Priestley*

Tuesday, 30th November, was the day of Petrina's second therapy session. The first thing I did in the morning when I reached my workplace was to update Beatrice on the things that had been happening to Petrina. We had a habit of sharing therapy experiences with each other.

She replied instantly. Interestingly, she had additional details about Petrina's spouse: "She is indeed a brave girl. Very traumatic experience, and a good thing that she ends up in your clinic. At least she will get better after the sessions. With all these traumatic experiences, medicine can't remove the trauma, can it? The husband depended on her when he was taking his Diploma Course. After completion, he found a better paying job but couldn't take the stress, and resigned. He stayed at home like a useless bum, drinking and smoking. She must have that sense of being betrayed when her husband has another woman after sacrificing so much for him."

*****

I had specially set aside time that morning for Petrina. At around 11:00 am, she came to my clinic, accompanied by her mother. Although elegantly dressed she looked somewhat pale and haggard. Her mother introduced herself, handed Petrina over to my care and then hurriedly excused herself to go to work.

Inside the consultation room, she updated me on what had happened last night. She recalled having another blackout shortly after she phoned me during dinner. As she was about to lapse into sleep, she heard a short hypnagogic conversation between herself and an identified man:

(Man): "You are the last one that I'll hurt."

(Petrina): "You promised that you'd never hurt me but you did it again."

After she woke up, she started to experience a loss of memory. The mysticism underlying her condition seemed to be building up. I wondered if this dialogue could provide an important clue to her underlying amnesia.

I asked if the unidentified man could be her husband and she firmly replied that it was most unlikely. This implied she might have another lover that had complicated her story, but she was not in a mental state to help me put the jigsaw puzzle together. Instead, I thought I might assist her recovery of memory of the identity of this "mystery" man using hypnotherapy.

Petrina was now ready for her second therapy session. The moment she was under trance, I asked: "What emotion is associated with your latest blackout?"

"Disappointment and frustration," she whispered.

I deepened her trance state as I asked her to focus on these two emotions. "Go back to the last time you experienced disappointment and frustration and tell me what happened."

Amazingly she regressed back to a past event very much more quickly compared to the day before.

"I can see Fabian," she began softly.

"Tell me about him," I prompted.

"Sad …! We took sleeping pills together."

I was startled. Who was this Fabian? I was not aware of this part of her history. I decided to go with the flow of the story.

"Where are you now and what has happened?"

"I'm at home. I feel nauseated … can't wake up next morning. I've tried to commit suicide."

"Who is Fabian?" I asked, wondering if he could be the unidentified man in the hypnagogal dialogue that she had earlier talked about before she went into trance.

"He is a gay friend," she whispered. I was startled again.

"Fabian's mother was angry with me … I did not manage to see Fabian at the funeral. He took sleeping pills and died. I did not go to hospital … and I survived."

I subsequently found out that Petrina and Fabian were very close friends and they used to go shopping together frequently. Fabian was a homosexual who dressed up as a girl. He had contracted HIV from his male partner, who had since left him for another girlfriend. He was very depressed. As a result of the similarity in their predicaments and the parallel in their emotional crises, they planned to commit a simultaneous suicide. It was decided that each of them would do it separately in their respective residences. They each swallowed ten tablets of a sleeping medication as planned.

Fabian died from the overdose but Petrina survived the ordeal. Petrina had a past experience of experimenting with various types and dosages of psychoactive drugs when she was young. Presumably she survived because she had developed a better tolerance. Still, she experienced severe nausea and vomiting the next morning and had to see a general practitioner to obtain some anti-emetics.

"What happened after you survived?"

"I called Aaron … but he rejected my call," she said in an agitated and sorrowful voice. "I cannot recall what happened after that."

It wasn't clear to me at this stage how Aaron might fit into the picture. Nor was it obvious why Petrina would choose him to call at this stage. Again I decided to just go with the flow.

"Move to the next event that is associated with your emotion of disappointment."

There was a pause, and then she responded.

"Empty promises ..." she said, sounding very cynical. However, the story seemed to pick up momentum quickly.

"What is happening?" I asked.

"I am speaking to a man ... don't know who he is. I am at the void deck ... Oh!" She opened her eyes and snapped out of hypnosis suddenly.

It was disappointing, especially when the story was about to become intriguing. I wondered who this mysterious man could be and how he could be related to the "empty promises" that Petrina talked about.

Petrina had become fully conscious now, but I was determined to continue the session. With her consent I put her down into a trance state once more.

"I'm in bed, feeling very tired." Petrina started again.

"Is it daytime or night time?"

"It's daytime."

"What happened next?"

"I just went to sleep ... I see Aaron ... I do not know where he is ... (pause) I am asleep now.

"Fast forward the scene to the point when you wake up."

"I'm awake now ... Oh! Someone is coming in!"

Petrina suddenly opened her eyes, looking startled, and came out of trance. She was however unable to make out the identity of the person who startled her. This was puzzling.

I instructed Petrina to close her eyes again and relax. She went into trance once again.

"Focus your mind on the feeling of being trapped, and your thought of not having a choice ..." The sensory clues seemed to work very fast.

"I am having a conversation with someone on the phone."

"Who is he?" I asked curiously.

"I don't know."

"What is going on?"

"I am still married ... it's over ... Marriage is over. There is nothing more between us. My husband beats me up."

"What happened next?"

"Somebody says: It's just a piece of paper. You should protect yourself. He has no right to beat you. I'll always be around for you."

"Who is he?"

"I don't know his name ... Oh! It's Aaron." Petrina snapped out of hypnosis for the third time, and I noticed that it was at the mention of Aaron.

Fully conscious by now, Petrina got up from her couch. She sensed the perplexity on my face and offered to explain. "I feel very frustrated on hearing the word 'Aaron' every time, but I cannot recall who he is."

I remembered that Aaron was the name of her "psychologist" friend who had helped her in her difficult times when she was undergoing divorce, but it seemed that Petrina's memory of this man had been waxing and waning.

"From my contact list I am not able to trace who he is. Since September this year, after I attempted suicide with the sleeping pills, the name 'Aaron' keeps coming up, and each time I experience a blackout when I hear it."

As she explained, it became clearer that there was indeed a second man in her life. I began to speculate that this man was instrumental in triggering her memory blackouts.

In recent months Petrina had been examining some photographs of her own to help herself recall the identity of Aaron. Intriguingly she had repeatedly and unconsciously been travelling to a particular place in the Hougang area to search for clues, in the hope of recollecting who this person might be. In addition there was a management training company by the name of PEACE Consulting Services which always flashed into her mind whenever Aaron's name was mentioned. She had been calling up this company to obtain information on Aaron, but was told that Aaron no longer worked there.

"There is a special place in Hougang Avenue 3 that I go to recall my relationship with Aaron, and my friend Bernard is the one who drives me there." I listened attentively, wondering who Bernard was. She later explained that Bernard was a work colleague who was working with the Informatics Department of the hospital. Petrina had known him for more than a year and found him very helpful as a friend.

"Bernard tells me that I am not ready to recall Aaron's identity," she said with a dreamy stare in her eyes.

"Does Bernard know exactly who Aaron is?" I asked.

"Not sure. I have a feeling that I did not tell Bernard everything about Aaron and he does not know my purpose of going to this particular place repeatedly. Each time I go there, I will feel happy initially, but after a while, I start to experience frustration ... and I don't know why."

Petrina paused. There was obviously something very crucial about the identity of this person called Aaron whom she had been trying to recall but ended up feeling very desperate each time her attempt at recollection failed.

"Fifth of July is the date that keeps bumping into my head, and I do not understand why. I have a box at home where I kept old movie tickets, and one of them shows the date as 5 July 2010. Each time I look at that ticket, I have a kind of feeling that I cannot explain. I will start feeling breathless and suffocated. It is very complicated. Also whenever I hear the name of this training organization called PEACE Consulting Services, I will have the same feeling as when I see the movie ticket. Whenever this company conducts the Silver or the Bronze Talk in the Ophthalmology Department, I get this same feeling of being suffocated and trapped."

I seemed to have come to a road block with this young lady. From her story, this person Aaron seemed to be the key to her loss of memory, but his identity remained a mystery.

Petrina sighed. "One part of me wants to find out who Aaron is and what role he plays in my life, but another part of me says 'no' and it is better not to know ..." She stared at me pathetically, and added: "I don't know what to do."

I looked intensely at her in silence. She seemed to have trapped herself in an inner conflict psychically. On my part I needed more time to mull over her problem and plan her future therapy sessions.

By then it was 1:15 pm, and I called the session to a close. I comforted her that things would straighten out eventually. As I watched her leaving in her brother's car I quietly prayed that she would rest well at home for the rest of the day.

Unfortunately Petrina experienced another blackout that afternoon. This time the blackout was triggered by a specific individual. Her supervisor, Shirlene, had called her at home demanding to know the details of her medical condition. As a supervisor, she felt she had every right to know the medical reasons for her subordinate's leave and whether, from a supervisor's perspective, those reasons were of sufficient gravity to justify one month of absence from work.

Petrina rejected her demand immediately because she considered that an intrusion of privacy. Why should she be divulging her personal medical information, which was confidential anyway? In the process of managing Shirlene's request she gave her my mobile number. She told Shirlene to call me instead. Not getting what she wanted, Shirlene threatened to accompany Petrina to my clinic on her next appointment to obtain the medical information. That threat was too much for Petrina. She fainted immediately. The moment she recovered, she called me.

"Hi, Dr. Mack. I had one short blackout after talking to my supervisor, Shirlene. She has threatened me. I've a very frustrating feeling the moment I hear her name but can't recall anything about what happened ..." She sobbed.

Shirlene was the same supervisor who had adamantly rejected Petrina's application for unpaid leave earlier in May 2010. Apparently, she herself was a divorcee. Based on her personal experience she did not feel the need for Petrina to take leave to settle a divorce.

I mused over Shirlene's style of management that evening. Although I had never met her in person, it was obvious that commanding and controlling subordinates was part of her agenda and this involved the use of denigrating comments and threats. Probably belonging to the *Napoleon archetype*, I thought. She seemed to love tearing other people down to make herself look good. I was not sure of the extent to which she had contributed to Petrina's emotional trauma, but her ability to precipitate a syncope on Petrina's part did sound formidable. Perhaps facets of this interpersonal conflict would soon surge from Petrina's unconscious mind at a future therapy session.

Chapter Five

Repressed Memory

The repressed memory is like a noisy intruder being thrown out of the concert hall. You can throw him out, but he will bang on the door and continue to disturb the concert. The analyst opens the door and says, If you promise to behave yourself, you can come back in.

— Theodor Reik

It was Wednesday, and I was running my weekly outpatient clinic again. I had rescheduled my surgical clinic to finish by around 3:00 pm. This would give me the needed time to conduct a third therapy session with Petrina in the afternoon.

It was lunch hour and I set aside some quiet moments to myself. While reflecting over what happened during yesterday's session, I recalled Petrina describing a significant inner conflict within herself. A part of her wanted badly to know the identity of Aaron because the knowledge thereof was crucial to her memory recovery and wellbeing. Yet, another part of her was filled with a fear of the unknown, and was afraid of the price to pay for uncovering the truth.

My mind drifted back to my earlier training days when I was taught that those patients who experienced inner emotional conflicts would make ideal candidates for "parts therapy", a special hypnotherapy approach. The parts-therapy technique involves the use of direct communication between the therapist and certain parts of the patient's unconscious mind that are involved in helping to achieve a conflict resolution. These parts could assume different personae under a trance state.

The existence of the so-called "parts" within us is because various models of our universe color our perception of life and influence our way of being. For each of these models, we may develop a corresponding self-image and a set of feelings, behavior, beliefs and body gesture. Each of these constellations of elements constitutes a kind of miniature subpersonality within us, which hypnotherapists call a "part". In fact, these subpersonalities are psychological satellites, coexisting as a multitude of lives within the milieu of our overall personality.

I had once discussed the concept and application of "parts therapy" with a psychiatrist colleague and he strongly supported its use. His experience was that if the technique was appropriately applied it could save the psychotherapist many months of psychoanalysis work.

Petrina turned up at 3:20 pm in my clinic. I spent a good fifteen minutes explaining to her about the technique. While speaking to the parts could be a fascinating process for the therapist, it could potentially be a very frightening experience for the unprepared patient. During parts therapy, each "part" of the patient's subconscious mind could take on a different persona, and, as such, different parts might speak in different tones, even though it was through a common voice box.

I brought Petrina rapidly down into a somnambulistic state of hypnosis and managed to call out two parts. There was a conflicting part that was masculine in nature and a motivating part that was feminine. The conflicting part did not want Petrina to recall her memory and named itself as LOST. The motivating part, who called itself HAPPY, was keen that she regained her memory early so that she could be happy. Between these two parts, Petrina and myself, the "four" of us held a short and intriguing discussion.

Dr. Mack: Hello. Is there is a part of Petrina that does not want her to recall her lost memories? If you are there I would like to talk to you.

Conflicting Part: I am here.

Dr. Mack: What is your name please?

Conflicting Part: Call me Lost. [Masculine tone]

Dr. Mack: Hi, Lost! Are you male or female?

LOST: I am male.

Dr. Mack: How long have you been in Petrina?

LOST: Since she was six years of age.

Dr. Mack: What role do you play inside Petrina?

LOST: Petrina is lonely and helpless. She wants attention. Her dad likes to gamble and Petrina is always angry. She is not well now. I am here to help her.

Dr. Mack: How do you propose to help her, now that she has lost her memory of Aaron?

LOST: [Pause] Well … Aaron is a nice man. He loves his family and he cares for her. He has his own company called Marissa Professional Cleaners. He is 27 to 28 years old and unmarried. Petrina does not want the relationship and wants to be loyal to the husband. Petrina likes him but she knows she can't continue with him. Aaron chooses to end the relationship and Petrina objects to it.

Dr. Mack: Hi, Petrina. Why did you object to the decision?

Petrina: I have no choice … I went into depression and tried to commit suicide because of Aaron.

Dr. Mack:	Now, I want to speak to that part of Petrina who is keen to help her to recover her lost memories and make her happy. Are you there?
Motivating Part:	Yes, I'm here. [feminine voice]
Dr. Mack:	What name do you want to be called?
Motivating Part:	Call me Happy.
Dr. Mack:	Happy, how do you think you can help Petrina?
HAPPY:	Well, Petrina is keen to recover her lost memory but Lost is against it because Lost thinks it is too painful and probably good for her to forget it altogether.
Dr. Mack:	But what is your view? Don't you think one way for Petrina to regain happiness is to regain her memory?
HAPPY:	Yes, but Petrina herself does not want to meet Aaron.
Dr. Mack:	Petrina, can you speak to me and tell me why is this so?
Petrina:	[Pause] I tried calling him the day after I attempted suicide … but he rejected my call.

From this short conversation, Petrina's story appeared to be building up in complexity and suspense. What had become clearer now was that the decisive factor in her suicide attempt in September did not reside entirely with Joshua. Enough evidence had surfaced now to suspect that Aaron had a significant role in it. Unfortunately, Petrina's internal conflict had not been resolved within this session. Unconsciously she stayed firm with not wanting to confront Aaron. I was speculating that the reason was because Petrina had experienced some very painful memories with the man, and these were too traumatic to pursue. The session ended at this point after I integrated the two parts back into Petrina.

After emerging from trance, Petrina recalled that she had always been drawn by a tendency to repeatedly surf an Internet website called "Marrisa Professional Cleaners" but never had the faintest idea of the underlying reason until now. For the first time, I deeply appreciated what Petrina meant when she described her feeling as "being stuck".

I called for a break to let her adjourn to the washroom. Upon her return, I offered to continue the therapy.

Petrina was brought down into trance again, and this time she regressed back to her working place in the Ophthalmology Clinic with her supervisor, Shirlene. I guided her imagery initially but she very quickly took on a narrator's role.

"She is a tyrant ... forces people to do things that they do not want to."

"Where are you now?"

"I am at the clinic, running the bills. The clinic ended. I have a whole stack of bills needing to be run. It is already 8:30 pm ..." She paused.

Petrina used to work in a beauty parlor for a big business organization and she did well as a sales manager. However, with the stress of her marriage failure and her declining physical stamina she chose to leave the company at the beginning of 2010 to work at a hospital clinic for lower pay. The patient reception area in the clinic had two sets of counters – patient registration and payment counters. To my knowledge, the workload at the front counter could be extremely heavy during peak hours.

"I am still at the clinic." She sighed. "My husband called me. He is waiting for me outside. He wants me to sign a paper to say that he will not pay me anything after the divorce." Her eyes started to well up.

"I am so busy. There are some other clerks sitting at the counter ... and they could get help ... but I am left alone." Tears were rolling down her cheek. "Joshua is forcing me to leave ... but there is so much to do. I can't leave ... I still have to call patients for their next appointment dates. Why is it that with the other two clerks sitting at the counter they will not help? Just because their supervisors are of the same ethnic group?" She started crying.

"It is my job ... I agree I have to do it, but I don't agree with the fairness they are giving. It is just that the other billing clerk did not do her job well and the queue has built up. There are 300 patients ... only two billing counters. I don't understand ... there are only 20 registrations and they don't need three registration counters ... One of them should switch to billing. I am doing it all alone ..." Her voice carried distress.

"What happened next?"

"Joshua is forcing me. I have to go. No one bothers to help ... There is no teamwork. I broke down. They called my supervisor. I told her I can't come to work tomorrow ... physically and emotionally drained. I need to take leave. My supervisor says: Why don't you come back tomorrow and we talk? Just give me one week to solve my physical and emotional problems and I will come back to work ... It's different. Her husband did not betray her ... did not beat her. How to compare? It is only one week of leave ... and so hard to get." Her voice was distressed. "I told her that if that is the case I will tender my resignation. One month's notice and I rest at home ... day after tomorrow.

"I went back ... she says the same thing. I am so tired. No choice. I want to take one week leave to settle the divorce. She will not help me ... I can't do it. She hates me ... she says I threaten her. She says: 'If you threaten me I will fire you. You trust me, focus on your work and you will be alright.'"

"I started to black out more often. Lunch time blackout has always been consistent. I request to transfer out of the subsidized clinic to somewhere lighter.

"I need the leave ... I need rest." A tone of despair was present in her voice. "She called me to her room. She says she is disappointed. 'Your performance goes down the drain,' she says. I tried to argue with her. [pause] I need to rest. I hate to think that she forces me. Just one week leave ... so hard. I need the rest so much. I told her because I foresee my personal issues have affected me. I cannot focus. Why is it not approved? If it affects the bonus so be it! I am tired ... I need a rest. Her answer is still no." Petrina started sobbing.

"My lunchtime is 1:00 to 2:00 pm. Sometimes it is only half an hour. Once there are 50 patients and only one temporary staff who doesn't know anything. I have to handle it all alone. I tell myself I can handle it, but why am I working so hard? Nobody is going to appreciate. I will never, ever beg anybody for just one week ... so difficult to get unpaid leave. I told her I want a different way of handling stress. Let me go for a short holiday and sort out my own emotional problems and I will come back ... She did not bother. I start to wonder ... should I be the one being disappointed with her?

"I have to put on a smile and go to work. I can't tell my mum about it. Have to face my dad (stepfather) as well.

"I fainted outside the cancer center. She (Shirlene) said: 'You are spoiling yourself. You cannot blame anyone for what happens today!' At that time I had just had an abortion. I need rest. She says: 'I did similar things before and I still come to work. I can do it, you can do it. I have been through it.'

"I told myself ... Why not just rest and do not wake up? I am so tired. The pay is so low and she expects me to work such long hours. She says: 'Your previous job was twenty-four seven,' ... But it is $2100 in the previous job versus $1300 in my present salary. I don't want overtime ... Unpaid leave not approved.

What should I do? She conceded she is the one putting pressure on me."

At this point Petrina went into a full catharsis.

I allowed a couple of minutes for Petrina to go past her emotional peak. I had learned from my training days that emotional distress, if not expressed, would get stored and build up pressure in the body's system. The greater the expression of negative emotions, the greater the experience of symptom relief would be.

Intensive regression therapy had been tough going for both Petrina and me. I called the session to an end. We felt that we both needed a break and we mutually agreed to resume therapy early next week.

What had been worrying me was that Petrina's fainting spells had persisted despite the intensity of the therapy. In that respect, I thought I needed to figure out a way of monitoring the frequency and gravity of her blackouts. I asked her if she could do me a favor by charting her syncopal attacks so that I would have a record of her progress. She surprised me by saying that she had a habit of keeping a journal since young and she could easily record not only her blackouts but note down all her relevant symptoms and feelings in addition. I was exhilarated. Journal keeping would likely be a useful companion for her healing journey. The act of making journal entries would provide room for expressive writing which in turn could stimulate her awareness and mental clarity. Ultimately this would give form and meaning to her feelings. At once I strongly encouraged her to continue with the habit. Now she would have a place to record her feelings which might be too painful or too shameful to share with others.

Petrina revealed that with her recent deterioration in health, her practice of journal keeping had been discontinued, but it was meant to be a temporary interruption. In fact she had recently burned her previous volume of her diary because she badly wanted to exclude certain individuals from her memory. However, she had no issue resuming her journal keeping. After all, her loss of memory had been so socially incapacitating that she felt the need to document some of her daily events and feelings as a reference source to fall back on whenever she needed help for recall. As an ongoing account of her experiences and feelings, I felt that it would provide the place for her to record the steps that she would be taking to help herself.

It was 5:50 pm. I ended the session and, like the previous day, accompanied Petrina to the car pick-up point. Despite the fact that she had just gone through a heavy catharsis, she was able to bring together a smile before departing.

Chapter Six

Voice Within

Life is difficult.
This is a great truth, one of the greatest truths.
It is a great truth because once we truly see this truth,
we transcend it.
Once we truly know that life is difficult –
once we truly understand and accept it –
then life is no longer difficult.
Because once it is accepted,
the fact that life is difficult no longer matters.
– M. Scott Peck

The next four days of her life turned out to be a very trying time for Petrina, both emotionally and physically. Although resting at home, she was continually bombarded with flashbacks. She had bought a new diary book and recommenced her journal keeping. This was a blessing as now I could track her clinical progress efficiently.

On Thursday morning, 2nd December, at 7:30 am, Petrina woke up feeling giddy and nauseated. She had a light breakfast at around 9:00 am. As the feeling of nausea did not go away, she went back to bed. Just before she lay down on the bed she heard a ringing sound in both her ears again. She lay down on the bed at once. The next thing she heard before she experienced another blackout were the following words:

"Petrina, it's you that have been harping on it! I told you many times I can do it, you can do it too! All the health issues you have right now are caused by yourself, what you went through I went through the same thing before! All these are eating you up! By doing all these it will affect your performance! I'm very disappointed in you! Taking rest will not help you; the leave will not help you! Trust me that you can do it without the leave. You can't allow yourself to have time to think about it; it will soon be over!"

The voice sounded very familiar and it seemed to belong to her supervisor Shirlene. She disliked the voice. "It makes me feel frustrated, helpless and trapped, as if I am forced to do things I don't want to ..." she wrote in her diary.

Shortly after listening to the voice, Petrina dipped in her conscious state and lapsed into a deep sleep for several hours. She woke up at 2:00 pm feeling very lost. She could neither recall anything of the past three therapy sessions nor her supervisor Shirlene. She was very frustrated and worried that her condition had made a turn for the worse. She called me to share her depressed feelings. As before, I made it a point to infuse hope, reassuring her that her condition was under control and needed time to improve.

Things brightened up. At 2:30 pm, congratulatory telephone calls were coming in to her from her colleagues. The Human Resource Department had recently held its first "Mystery Shopper" Staff Awards for excellence in service. Apparently Petrina was an award winner and her photograph had been put up on the walls everywhere at the Ophthalmology Clinic. For a moment she felt so happy about her work achievement that she forgot about her earlier frustration.

Fifteen minutes later she received a congratulatory email with an attached photo from a colleague. As she opened up the attached picture file, all her frustration, anger, trapped feelings and helplessness came back!

It so happened that there were two award winners, the other winner being her supervisor, Shirlene. The irony of the situation was that the two personal photographs were posted side by side in an announcement! Petrina passed out at the sight of it.

I was both concerned and frustrated. Each new syncope might carry with it the morbidity of further loss of short-term memory. Furthermore each new blackout seemed to perpetrate an added sense of hopelessness, as though all her efforts at therapy had gone to waste.

By 6:45 pm she woke up feeling much better. Still she could not recall anything much, not even what she had for breakfast that morning. She was afraid and began wondering if she might start to forget everyone and everything eventually. She opened her diary and began writing again. Some of her relevant journal entries are reproduced as blocks of italicized text below and in subsequent pages of this book.

Thursday, *2 December*
⇨ *11:45 pm*
I'm still awake and afraid of going to sleep and wake up the next morning losing memory again ... Listening to my favorite music hoping to recall my past memory as I always do everyday before I go to bed. My body and mind are feeling very tired but somehow have no idea how without sleeping pills and anti-anxiety medicine, I can sleep. It's been 3 years since I have really slept. I'm starting to wonder would it be a better option to really go into a deep sleep state; at least that's the time where I can really get the rest I want. On the other hand when I think of my family and I've got to explore a lot of things in the world I can't give up ... feel lost, don't want to think of anything, wanted to cry out, nothing come out ... unable to cry like when I was younger.

This is not me. I want to find the confident happy, positive Petrina but as days passed I start to feel that my memory is losing more and seems like I'm getting worse.

*May be I just can't relax, can't find the inner peace in me.
Just pray hard that tomorrow I can wake up with no
further memory loss again.*

Petrina did not sleep well that night and was woken up twice by
two different voices. At around 4:00 am she heard a man's voice
that sounded like her husband saying:

"I no longer love you! The reason why I'm stuck with you is
because of your money, stupid woman!"

At 7:00 am next morning she woke up again feeling very
giddy and nauseated. She retched but nothing came out. It was a
terrible time. For the rest of the day she had to struggle against
sleep disturbance from auditory hallucinations.

At about 10:00 am she was woken up again by the voice of
Shirlene telling her about the disappointment her supervisor had
in her performance. This voice message added significantly to her
mental pressure because she was feeling that she was already
bearing a very heavy emotional burden. Shortly after that, before
she fell asleep she heard a masculine voice saying: "Petrina, you
are tired ... you should let go ... Let yourself go into deep
sleep ..."

Petrina woke up at around 2:00 pm feeling very sleepy on top
of being giddy and nauseated. These symptoms deterred her from
smoking and she thought it might be a good thing for her. She
went back to sleep again and woke up at around 9:30 pm, still
feeling very tired.

She did not have a good-quality sleep. She could hear her
mother packing in her bedroom and living room even while she
was supposedly asleep. Later that evening, her mum told her
some bad news about her Aunt Jasmine (Fig. 1). Her aunt's
medical condition had deteriorated. She had been suffering from
advanced breast cancer, and now a metastatic spread of her cancer
cells to other body organs had taken place. She had declined
chemotherapy for reasons of cost, preferring to save the money

for her children's education. This was depressing. Petrina felt that too many unhappy events were happening at the same time.

*****

On Saturday, Petrina woke up at 7:00 am with a heavy heart. She experienced flashes of images of Joshua and Hazel.

Hazel was a Eurasian girl who had been her best friend until she realized that she had had an affair with Joshua. After that, Hazel decided to migrate to Canada. Petrina had remained in the dark all the time and even went to her house to help her pack for her trip. While packing in her bedroom she unintentionally spotted a photograph showing her husband and Hazel intimately together. From that moment onwards, she realized that her friendship had been betrayed. Since then, whenever she talked about the discovery of that particular photograph of Hazel and Joshua, she would get very emotional.

Next she experienced another flashback of herself pleading unsuccessfully with Shirlene to approve her unpaid leave to rest at home. It was the first time in her life that she put down her dignity to beg for help and yet she was turned down. It was also the first time she had broken down emotionally at the workplace.

Saturday, 4 December
⇨ *7:10 am*

I could recall that I'm not a person who will drop a single tear in front of people who are not close to me. Yet with all the pressure I've been through I thought it's time to get a rest, I still have a long way ahead of me. It's been very tiring to put on a mask to work smiling but I feel sad, frustrated, lost and helpless.

Guess indirectly Shirlene has been adding pressure on me unknowingly. Maybe she meant well but not everyone can face and handle the stress the same way she did. Thinking of that, all the frustration and emotional instability comes back again ... To me her so-called care and concern is just to show other staff she cares but seems like very fake to me!

I've come to a point where it's not worth making myself so miserable. Why not just forget about everything, don't think of anything. Since I can't get a solution ... I've to move on. Be it I like it or not, that's life.

At around 9:00 am, Petrina tried calling her step-aunt. Earlier on, her mum had asked her to collect a movie ticket and she wanted to confirm if her aunt was coming. However, all of a sudden, she had forgotten her purpose of calling and felt that she could no longer recognize her. This worried her. Next she rationalized to herself. It was probably because she didn't see her often enough, she thought. Unfortunately, the ringing sound in her ears suddenly started again and she had another blackout.

This time the blackout lasted two and a half hours and no one in the house noticed it. Her brother was soundly asleep all the while. She subsequently woke up at around 11:50 am in the living room with a bad headache and a feeling of weakness. However, she could still remember certain things and she therefore comforted herself that she might be on her way to recovery.

Petrina was staying in the same room as her second brother in a crowded apartment. He was working in Human Resources, and had taken up further studies leading to a degree course. She was supposed to wake him up for his classes that afternoon but to her dismay, she had totally forgotten!

Saturday, *4 December*
⇨ *3:02 pm*
Kinda feeling unstable, don't like the feeling. The more I tell myself I want to recall my memory, seems like I start to forget. Maybe I'm giving myself too much pressure.

By now I had realized that Petrina was someone who would not easily give up. She had a lot of resilience and seemed to be able to weather storms courageously. She had the habit of updating me regularly on her clinical status through SMS messages and I frequently took the opportunity to infuse hope in my responses. At 6:40 pm I sent Petrina a message.

"Good evening ... I believe that any improvement on your part, big or small, is a major step forward. Keep up your spirits. Be sure that you will recover, and soon enough to return to work."

"Thank you, Dr. Mack. I will get better."

Things seemed to be turning the corner later in the evening. By 9:00 pm Petrina's sense of wellbeing had improved. She was wide awake and, surprisingly, not tired at all. She was free from giddiness. At last she enjoyed a feeling of being back to normal. Things became more upbeat.

The clock chimed. It was 3:00 am. She remained wide awake with no sense of sleepiness. For a moment she was not sure if it was because she had been sleeping too much in the day or because she had been conditioned with the fear of losing further memory each time on waking up from sleep.

She took out her photo album and ruminated over her broken relationship with Joshua. She was saddened by the outcome of her marriage and the resulting decline in her health. Nothing that she had done so far seemed to have changed things. She "felt trapped" in a situation where the cost of altering the course of her life seemed too high. She felt as if she was in a prison without parole.

Later as she was mourning over her failed marriage, she started to draw (Fig. 2). I had earlier encouraged her to exercise her skills in artistic expression in the hope that it would give her an opportunity to vent her emotions. I had learned from previous training that the process of representing one's emotions with expressive art carries therapeutic value in itself. Little did I realize that this process would turn out to be a powerful therapeutic tool in her recovery.

Fig. 2: "Beautiful yet broken"

Many of Petrina's expressive drawings are reproduced in this book because they represented her mood fluctuations very accurately. As I followed her in my clinic each time, I soon discovered that some of these art pieces had been products of her unconscious mind and had symbolic significance embedded in them. I had previously wondered how best I could understand her inner world, and it seemed now that I had encountered a feasible method.

Fig. 3: "A wish that will not come true"

In the quiet of the morning, as Petrina was expressing her emotions in art form, she felt a sense of uncertainty. It was like Demeter in Greek mythology who was wandering in fruitless search for her lost daughter Persephone. She had been depressed over her decision of marrying early and was unsure what to do with her life henceforth. The dysfunctional relationship between her parents dismayed her from a young age and she had been hoping to provide a contrast by securing a blissful marriage for herself early in her life.

She and Joshua were teenage friends and had known each other for thirteen years, as they lived in the same neighborhood. Despite many quarrels and splits they eventually decided that they were destined for each other and got married. She had never dreamed that her marriage would end up in a wreck.

What was notable at this stage was the way she remarked about her regret over her comparative relationship with Aaron vis-à-vis her husband.

Sunday, 5 December
⇨ *2:52 am*

I'm looking again at my Registry of Marriage photos. My heart feels as if I'm bleeding internally the emotion is so strong, quite similar to Aaron, but somehow just feel slight difference ... Towards my ex-husband I felt betrayal kind of feeling but Aaron is just like full of regrets. Tried not to think of Aaron but somehow the past few hours I have flashes of images of me and a very tall, tanned man. None of my friends look like that ... Was it my imagination or is this man Aaron? Thinking of him I'm having the giddiness again ...

The exact nature of her relationship with Aaron was still unknown to me at this stage but turned out to be something that she and I had to jointly unravel over the course of the next week.

61

As she was finishing off the last sentence in the early hours of the morning she started experiencing a ringing sound in her ears again. Giddiness came on and it was followed by a man's voice saying: "You are the last one that I'll ever hurt." Following that she heard herself replying: "But you've already hurt me!" This dialogue sounded familiar – it seemed identical to the dialogue that I had earlier heard from Petrina.

What followed immediately after this was the voice of her supervisor, reprimanding her for having brought her health issues upon herself. Shirlene's voice continued to have a very negative impact. This time, on hearing the voice Petrina experienced another blackout lasting seven hours. She lapsed into a deep sleep and when she woke up at around 10:00 am the next morning she was afraid to let her mum know. Each time she heard Shirlene's voice or her name she would get very agitated and feel frustrated, angry, trapped and helpless (Fig. 4). This time round she felt more hopeful as she was able to still recall things after waking up.

Fig. 4: "When would she stop haunting me?"

Her experiences for the rest of the day were not pleasant. She continued to be emotionally haunted by voices. For a long time it was a commonly held idea that auditory hallucinations were pathological and indicative of mental illness. However, in the short space of time that I had been interacting with Petrina, I intuitively felt otherwise in her case. Interestingly, throughout her ordeal she had been able to identify her own inner voice among the various other voices she had captured.

Sunday, 5 December
⇨ *1:17 pm*

The past few hours I have been hearing voices. "Don't think of Shirlene. She is the one that adds on to your pressure. That caused you to come to this stage now and don't let her win. She's a hypocrite! She knows what you are going through but still gives you pressure."

Petrina stayed widely awake again until 1:00 am as she was bombarded with flashes of images in addition to voices. This time she had associated headaches. It was very tiresome, and she wondered when her ordeal would be over. She finally fell asleep and woke in good spirits at 9:20 am the following morning.

It was a bright sunny morning on Monday, 6 December. She was refreshed and cheerful and the turbulence of the mental experience of the day before was now behind her. She remembered she had an afternoon appointment with me for her fourth therapy session and she was looking forward to it.

She left her house early to go to the HR Department to settle some business. She remembered that over the weekend a colleague had called to congratulate her over her winning of a Client Service Award. She arrived at the HR Department of the hospital at around 1:00 pm to collect her prize – a $10 voucher. She picked up her pay slip at the same time. On the way she saw her photo was being displayed on all the lifts in the clinic block and felt very elated. However, inside a lift she saw Shirlene's photograph posted side by side with hers. This immediately triggered voices in her left ear and forewarned an impending syncope. Fortunately her mother was accompanying her and she managed to get over the symptom quickly without fainting. She briskly walked over to my clinic and at 1:45 pm she alerted me with a SMS message to herald her arrival.

She looked uneasy and I promptly helped her to a chair. Once inside my consultation room she shared with me one of her mental experiences over the weekend.

She'd had a "vision" of a man who was tall and tanned, walking into a movie theater. She was unsure of his identity. She referred back to her wedding photos and this man did not look like her husband. The description fitted that of Aaron, but she was not able to confirm it. Also, she had since located Aaron's name and telephone number on her computer database, but an inexplicable force was inhibiting her from calling him. She was simply not prepared to dial the number.

As I prepared the couch for the next therapy session, Petrina excused herself to go to the washroom. Several minutes later, I heard the noise of a fall just outside my consultation room.

My heart sank ...

Chapter Seven
Depths of Despair

Just as the body goes into shock after a physical trauma, so does the human psyche go into shock after the impact of a major loss.

– Anne Grant

At the sound of the noise, I hurried out of my room. Lo and behold, Petrina was lying on the floor of the corridor, unconscious and motionless. She had fallen prey to syncope. A commotion in the clinic quickly followed and several nurses were rushing to the spot.

For a couple of seconds, I was dumbfounded. Fortunately a fellow patient sitting in the waiting area had witnessed the blackout and saw her sinking to her feet, landing on the right shoulder. She assured me that Petrina did not hit her head in the process. I felt a little relieved.

She was quickly transferred to the examination couch and I did a brief clinical examination to make sure she had no obvious fractures or physical injuries from the fall. Thereafter I left her to rest. Her sensorium was slowly regaining clarity. In the meantime I reassured the nurses that this was not her first fainting episode and that she was already rapidly recovering.

Several thoughts crossed my mind as I waited. Petrina had had a rough weekend and had bravely weathered her emotional turmoil. She seemed to be experiencing a blackout every time just when improvement appeared to be in sight. I was feeling the pressure of the responsibility of looking after someone who needed dedicated attention and close monitoring. I had been rearranging my clinical schedule to cater to her healing needs. However, I was unsure if my stamina could outlast her ordeal!

Minutes passed … She gradually moved her limbs and opened her eyes slowly. It felt as if it took all afternoon.

After becoming fully composed, Petrina shared that she was experiencing a special feeling of "being suffocated" at the moment when she was feeling faint. After some deliberation, she decided that she still wanted the therapy session.

There was hesitancy on my part. Would it be in her interest to postpone the therapy to another day? However, she was firm. Moreover, her new symptom of "feeling suffocated" had intrigued me. Intuitively I felt that something of paramount significance was about to reveal itself. I agreed to proceed.

"Close your eyes and take a deep breath. Focus your conscious awareness on the emotion of suffocation …" I began softly.

As if like magic, Petrina went into a trance promptly, and quickly regressed back to a very startling event.

"He is beating me. It's Joshua …" Distress was in her voice.

"Tell me what happened."

"The belt …" Tears were welling up in her eyes. I was puzzled.

"He is whipping me with his belt …" she continued, which startled me. A story of brutal violence and physical abuse had just emerged and I was not expecting it.

"What happened next?"

"I can see Hazel and him together in bed. They betrayed me. I threw Hazel out of the house … I have done nothing wrong." Tears started to roll down the sides of her cheek.

"What are your emotions at this stage?"

"Hatred," she said firmly.

"What are your thoughts that go with the hatred?"

"I love him so much and he betrayed me." She started to cry.

In a flood of emotions, another story emerged.

"He used his belt to beat up my dog as well ... It's bleeding."

I later learned that Petrina had two pet dogs at home and one of them would come up to her pitifully each time after being beaten up. The other dog had run away from home since and was never found.

"What happened next?"

"He left home," she continued. "I went to call for help, but I don't want to get him into trouble. I thought if I give him a chance he will change. When he is angry he will use the belt to beat me up. He just wanted my money ... that's all. He did not come back ... and I waited." She was in catharsis.

"What did you do when he did not come back?"

"I went to Hazel's home. I saw them together in the void deck. I followed them to the car and asked them: 'Why?' ... She is driving the whole thing ... He says: 'I don't need you anymore.' I spent seven years in an empty marriage. He pushed my head against the car window. I started to bleed from the left side of my forehead ... I went back. I've never begged him once before like this." She continued to sob.

There was a long pause. She suddenly jumped to a different event.

"It's so much to go through. My supervisor is not helpful. She said to me: 'What you went through, I went through.' She does not understand. It's so hard to get a rest. It's better to sleep and not to wake up.

"She said I am useless. It is okay for me to do the work and you give me the leave, but you have no right to insult me. She said: 'You brought this upon yourself. It is your choice. Your fainting spell is caused by your own smoking too much. Don't put the blame on anybody.' She used very hurtful words.

"I have been working so hard for her and yet she does not appreciate me. I used to handle sixty to seventy registrations and billings without complaint. This is the way you repay me. I told her there is no junior clerk among you who can handle seventy patients like I do ... She says I threatened her. I told her that since you don't see the same point as I do, I want a transfer. She says: 'You have done this to yourself. You do not need the leave.' I start to wonder. What is the Ophthalmology Clinic for? Will it collapse in one week without one person? I see her selfishness. She only thinks of herself, making use of other people. She said: 'I am so disappointed with you. Your performance is going down the drain.'

"I have to put up a smile to go to work every day. I tend to make mistakes ... I am so tired. Do I have to go to the Ministry of Manpower to get the leave?" Her voice went into a decrescendo as she became visibly more desperate.

There was a long pause.

Then suddenly, crying away, she jumped back into her story with Joshua. "Oh ... Don't beat me! Joshua is beating me. I don't understand ..." Petrina snapped out of hypnosis with a fearful look on her face.

The emotional trauma sounded very deep; probably too painful to continue. I waited several moments for her to regain full consciousness before I started a conversation. She could remember every detail of what she had described under trance. In the conscious state she was able to fill in the gaps of her real life story.

She started to explain. "I forgot to wash his clothes one day and he tied me up on the bed to beat me," (Fig. 5) she said with a surprising calm. "I did not dare to go home to my mother's house for three years because of the belt. I don't want to report him to the police either. When he gets into trouble, my mother-in-law will also get into trouble. If he ever goes to jail my mother-in-law will collapse. She is old and Joshua knows my weak point.

"I left my husband and stayed with my mum since May 2010 because I cannot stand the pain anymore. My mother-in-law is eighty years old and she still has to work as a dish-washer in a restaurant to bring income home. She stays with Joshua. In recent months she has found out that Joshua has been beating me up. She suggested that I file a police report but I did not want to do so. She says she would rather stay alone than together with such a disgraceful son."

It was a heartbreaking story. It was difficult for me to envisage how someone could be so beastly in behavior towards his own spouse. I later learned that Joshua's sadistic practice went beyond the use of the belt. He used a baseball bat that had been pre-soaked in ice water and applied it to Petrina's skin wounds after he whipped her. She would suffer helplessly in pain. On some occasions he would forcefully put her hands in between blocks of ice and allowed her to scream in pain. Subsequently her skin would start peeling as a result of the cold injury.

Fig. 5: "I did not wash his clothes and he tied me up"

After drying her tears, Petrina seemed to have obtained a better insight into her own fear of the belt, and why she had the feeling of "being trapped". Before we ended the session, she opened her handbag and showed me her journal.

It was a beautiful hard-covered diary with a lovely and sentimental art pattern on the front. On the top left-hand corner of every page was a beautiful picture of a butterfly in purple. Her journal entries were made in nice, cursive handwriting, interspersed with hand-drawn sketches that represented her inner emotions. I couldn't help but reproduce many of her drawings in this book as they illustrate her inner world of feelings better than any words could describe.

I felt it was an effective way to facilitate Petrina's understanding of her inner psyche and pervasive sense of vulnerability through artistic expression. Her tendency to devalue her problem-solving ability had been working against her recovery process. The chance to explore her automatic thoughts and images through creative drawings had been helping her to construct her problematic situations and deal with her fears.

Monday, 6 December
⇨ *2 pm,*
Today I recalled how my ex-husband abused me by using a belt to beat me for not washing his clothes. All the pain, hatred and trapped feelings came back. I've always been afraid of belts but can't figure out why ... After today's therapy finally I get the answer. I've always felt trapped because the last time Joshua beat me ... he tied me to the bed ... He uses the belt to hit me. At that moment my feelings towards him was Love and Hate.

⇨ *8:45 pm*
I used to think that nothing's uncontrollable but seems like an emotion such as love is not something that can be controlled. When it comes to love there's no right or wrong ... Or maybe I shall put it this way, Does Love

exist in a relationship/marriage or it does not exist at all ...?

9:18 pm
Many say it's your choice to be happy or not but if they have got what I went through ... maybe they'll think like me. You must know what is "Let Go" before you can find happiness ...

At home that evening, after Petrina was well rested and in a relaxed mode, she came up with a most amazing drawing in her diary (Fig. 6). On completion of the drawing, she realized that one of the causes of her depression was that of her illusion – she had been holding on to something that was never there!

Fig. 6: "Holding on to something that was never there"

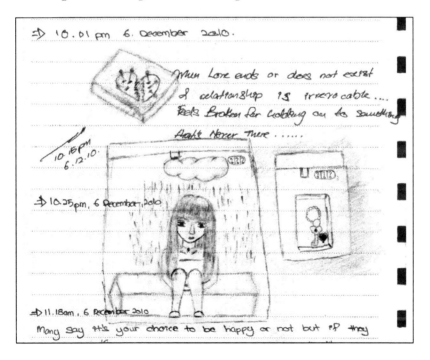

71

It was a picture of a young lady in a gloomy mood as represented by raindrops on a cloudy day. She was sitting down and brooding over her problems. On top of the picture was a drawing of a broken heart, fragmented into two, and nailed down with pins. She had hoped to achieve a successful marriage and love life that never existed between her parents. Through the act of drawing she had understood how her illusion came into being and how it functioned in her life. She could now detach herself from it and see it in action.

To one side of the picture was a drawing of a key placed in a box that was locked inside a safe with an unknown pass code. I was curious as to the meaning of the key inside the box but unfortunately, she couldn't tell me the significance behind that part of the sketch. What I also noticed was that the same picture of the key was sketched in an identical manner in another picture (Fig. 7). All she said was that she had drawn it out of her unconscious mind.

I was perplexed. The key does not conform to the usual appearance that we are aware of in modern life. Was there a symbolism behind it? Was there another layer of mystery within her inner psyche? Was another story waiting to come to light?

*****

Petrina spent most of her time sleeping on the Tuesday. Through an SMS message she reassured me that she had been able to obtain a slightly better quality of sleep after her therapy session the day before. This was partly because, after the re-living of the abusive experience with Joshua, she felt the emotional burden was now less.

She woke up at 7:00 am and heard her supervisor's voice again. It was very irritating because it kept haunting her. She wondered if and when that would ever end. By now it was clear that although Shirlene was one of the major contributors to her depression, her name no longer carried the power to trigger blackouts like it used to.

Despite her optimism, things did not seem to be all that well with her. She continued to experience suffocating and painful feelings with regards to what she had been going through. She drew a picture of herself crying in bed, a broken heart and a dangling sword pointing at her heart (Fig. 7). There were three lost kids crying out for their mummy. The inner guilt arising out of her three abortions seemed to be crying out from within. Her intrapsychic tension appeared to have come through in the medium of art.

Fig.7: "Suffocating and heart-piercing pain"

The picture, as I interpreted it, represented her insatiable need to repair and revive her loved ones. That had led to a state of mourning. I was concerned that her reparatory tendency might shift from a depressive guilt to a persecutory guilt that could be detrimental to her inner serenity; this needed working through or else it might become emotionally disabling.

Tuesday, 7 December
⇨ *7:45 am*
I had flashes of the images though I'm getting the rest at home but still feels suffocating and heart piercing pain,

unbearable pain ... I always wonder why there is so much trouble and problems and why not if I can't handle it just leave it aside since I can't find the solution, that way I'll be happier? But what is happy? Too long since I lost the feeling of happiness ... Lost track of it and have no idea where to find it. Recently I realize simplest things sometimes are the hardest things to get or achieve.

Working through her emotions would mean that she had to accept her loss in the first place. Only then would she be able to overcome her pathological defenses and re-adapt her ego to reality. The manner in which regression therapy could help in these processes would be to allow her to re-experience her traumatic events under trance, allowing her to reframe the experience in a different light.

Through her artistic creation, Petrina was working through her depressive state to recreate and restore the lost past. She appeared to be creating a world that seemed to simultaneously represent both her past and present. As I reflected on her drawings, I realized that an understanding of her past history served an important function of providing her with a sense of continuity in life.

Petrina felt asleep again later that morning, and woke up twice subsequently, once at 12:40 pm and again at 3:20 pm. On both occasions she felt very tired. She noticed that she had been experiencing this tired feeling every time after her therapy sessions. Psychically her shoulders felt lighter because she no longer sensed the heavy emotional burden that she had hitherto been carrying.

At 6:50 pm she woke up from her sleep in tears! This was the first time in Petrina's life that she had woken up crying. She'd had a very vivid dream in which she found herself locked inside in a room and a man was standing outside but unwilling to help her unlock the door. In her desperation to set herself free, she cried. Intuitively I interpreted it as if her inner self was sinking slowly into the depths of despair, while a trusted individual whom she had pinned her hopes on did not lift a finger to help her. In hindsight the vividness of the dream alerted me to the possibility of this being a karmic dream.

Fig. 8: "Unlock me, please!"

She had expressed the dream again in art form (Fig. 8). What was remarkable about the picture, and which I missed at first glance, was that the man in question wore a key around his neck. She had drawn the key unconsciously without understanding why she did it, but had made a special reference to it as the "key to her freedom" in her journal subsequently.

That evening, she suddenly felt that something or someone was missing in her life. It was such a lonely feeling that she drew a picture of herself standing isolated in a barren landscape, under a hot sun. She later explained to me that it was an expression of fear of finding herself alone and abandoned (Fig. 9). Her explanation made sense, because loneliness may indeed turn into a deadly abyss. However, I was hoping that she could see the two faces of solitude. If she could learn to confront her sense of aloneness and turn it into a feeling of uniqueness, she could develop a sense of infinite worth in her.

Fig. 9: "So alone ..."

Wednesday, 8 December
⇨ *1:20 am*

After Monday's therapy, though I've let out some emotion ...I feel much better but along with this somehow at the moment I'm as if very empty inside. Especially after I had the dream about me locked up in a room waiting for someone to unlock it and let me out ...

I refer back to the past two drawings – there's a key kept in a box and lock in a safe but I have no idea what is the pass code to unlock it. The man that I dreamt of is wearing the key around his neck ... Just can't help keep wondering is he the one that holds the key to my freedom or was it my imagination?

In my dream I also hear a man's voice telling me: "You are not the Petrina I know. You used to be very strong and positive ... the Petrina I see now is so fragile, weak and negative ..." The last three words I could recall Shirlene said the same thing to me. Until now Shirlene's voice still haunts me when I'm awake or asleep, but the voice can no longer make me feel as frustrated as before. That's a good sign but the anger is still there.

Little did I realize, at this point in time, that the "key" was an important karmic symbol, and the anchoring point of a most fascinating story that was to emerge and catch us by surprise in the days to come ...

Chapter Eight

Emptiness

*Once I knew only darkness and stillness ... my life was
without past or future ... but a little word from the fingers of
another fell into my hand that clutched at emptiness and my heart
leaped to the rapture of living.*

— *Helen Keller*

It was Wednesday, 8th December. Petrina arrived at my clinic at 3:15 pm for her fifth therapy session. This time she came unaccompanied because all her family members were at work.

Her previous sessions had been emotionally tough going but she was determined to persist and get well. She shared with me the information that the therapy had brought out her latest symptom of a feeling of "emptiness". Painful feelings had been interfering with her sense of wellbeing. This used up her energy and left her feeling drained and empty in addition to feeling alone. Somehow, she felt as if she was anticipating something important that was to happen soon and needed her attention.

She felt remorse after having gone through three abortions and her grief was expressed in relation to the hurting of her unborn babies. However, she understood that remorse could not annul "sin" and she could only sorrow over it. In fact she was harboring the thought that God might be punishing her now by making her feel lonely. She also recalled the comment from her gynecologist that she might not be able to conceive again in future because of her frequent, repeated abortions. That reinforced her sense of being punished at this stage. I mulled over this. Would it translate into a longing for reparation for her?

Wednesday, 8 December
⇨ *2:30 pm*

> *The feeling of emptiness, loss, being trapped and helpless has been with me for very long ... It never leaves me. Especially after Monday's therapy the feeling of emptiness is getting stronger. Joshua has taken most of what I have but what's left behind ... someone has taken the very last bit of what I have left. Now I feel like I'm a zombie? Or what's left behind is just empty shell.*
>
> *I've accepted and face the reality of what happened to my marriage, but starting all over again just seems hard. I'm afraid of losing and falling ... but I don't have a choice, I can only move on. Only by moving on then I believe I will reach my destination one day, otherwise I will always be here stagnant ...*

Petrina appeared tired and weary but keen as usual for the therapy. Upon a short induction, she went down into a trance state rapidly and I used her feeling of "emptiness" as the emotional bridge.

"I am waiting for Joshua," she mumbled. "Dinner is ready. He can come back and eat but he never comes back. This has happened countless times."

"What are your thoughts at this point?"

"It's an empty marriage. I waited more than five hours before he came home ... I sometimes wonder who is this man sleeping beside me? He says he has to work. But I know he is with Hazel. I took leave to follow him ... I found him in Hazel's house. He's kissing her."

"What are your emotions at this point?"

"Emptiness. I lost my friend. I lost my husband."

"What did you do when you saw him kissing Hazel?"

80

"I did nothing. They went into the house and came out after six hours. Then they went for dinner in a Japanese restaurant. I followed them. They looked so happy together ... but he never once brought me to any restaurant." Tears rolled down her cheeks.

"What happened next?"

"They did not know I was watching them. They went back to Hazel's home and he never came back. I stopped asking. I shut myself out. We quarrelled too many times because of Hazel. I stopped cooking for Joshua. He doesn't bother ... I don't want him to touch me ... He used force ... there is nothing I can do."

"What are your emotions at this point?"

"I feel lost."

"What thought goes with that feeling?"

"I thought maybe if he bothers to touch me he still loves me." She went into catharsis. There was a pause while she was struggling to get out of the emotional state.

"I started waiting for him again ... but I realize that I am just a sex machine to him. I lost everything. I just wish to move on. I told my mum that I am going for a divorce. She asked me to talk to him. I told my mum that I'd made up my mind and I'll go home soon.

"I started to receive a lot of calls from SingTel and StarHub chasing me for the debts that he incurred. I confronted him. He said: 'I never asked you to pay any of these bills. You did it willingly for me.'"

"How did you feel when he said that?"

"I expected it. He abused me. He would use the belt to beat me. He asked me to have sexual intercourse with him. I tried to push him away. He tied me to the bed ... I was bleeding." She went into catharsis again.

"After that I moved home. I lost everything. I did not talk to anyone. I kept everything to myself. I felt very pressurized.

There's nothing I can do. I have to move on. I kept myself busy. My working hours are getting longer."

Petrina paused for a moment, and then continued slowly and hesitantly. Suddenly she seemed to jump into another event.

"There is a man whom I was telling about Joshua at a restaurant. He looks familiar … in his late twenties but I cannot recall his name. He says Joshua has no right to do that to me."

I listened intently. Was she describing Aaron again?

"We left," Petrina continued.

"What happened next?"

"I see myself with a lot of blood. I cut my wrist." This caught my attention. This was the first time she had talked about wrist cutting. Later I learned that this took place before her attempted suicide with the sleeping pills.

Petrina continued: "I took sleeping pills … I am with Fabian. In my last conversation with Fabian, he says he is not coming back …" She ended with a note of sadness and then self-emerged from the trance state spontaneously.

I reflected over the session. The pattern of her response while under trance had been very consistent. Each time when either Aaron's name was mentioned, or a description of him came into the picture, Petrina would quickly snap out of hypnosis.

At this point, she was very tired and I decided to end the therapy session. She looked sorrowful and indicated that she was experiencing discomfort over her right upper chest. It was a twitching sensation and a feeling "as if she was being tied up".

Instinctively I laid my right palm over that spot. I had undergone training in Reiki healing several years before, and I use the modality as and when I discern a need in my patients. I felt the energy flowing instantly through my palms onto her chest and within seconds she fed back to me with a whisper: "It's warm!" What she felt was a form of healing energy. I left my hands there for the next several minutes as she became increasingly relaxed and lapsed into a dreamy state. Soon, a complexion of calm and peace radiated outwards from her.

The clinic assistant who acted as my chaperone was a middle-aged Indian lady. She asked me softly: "Doctor, you practice Reiki, don't you?"

I nodded my head and we smiled at each other. Later I found out that she had been in the company of friends who also practiced the art.

I had learned Reiki healing in early 2003. That was at a time when I felt that there was more to healing in medicine than just the practice of pharmacotherapy, surgery and radiation. I believed the universe had many other unexplored realms available for our healing needs.

Ten minutes passed. Petrina indicated that the pain over the chest was fading and the energy flow had diminished. I changed the positions of my hands to cover the other parts of her body, including her abdomen, mediastinum, and her head. The entire healing session lasted about 30 minutes and at the end of it, she lapsed into a state of sleep.

Petrina woke up 15 minutes later. With a tired smile she understood that the session had concluded and reassured me that she was ready to go home by herself. I then saw her off in a taxi.

*****

That evening, nightmares began again. Petrina had difficulty falling asleep. The moment she closed her eyes, she had flashes of frightening images of Joshua beating her up with a belt. The hypnotherapy session had revived one of the most traumatic memories in her marriage.

It was past midnight, and she was still struggling in bed. In the end she got up and wrote:

Thursday, 9 December
⇨ *12:38 am*

I can feel physical pain ... It's everywhere ... I'm afraid though Joshua can no longer hurt me. But after recalling he just seems to be haunting me ... There's nowhere I can hide ... feels like I'm shattered into pieces ... Have no idea how to pick myself up.

⇨ *1:45 am*

Still can't sleep. Out of sudden this thought came to my mind ... this journey of recovery is so painful ... if I have a choice I would rather not recall this particular part of the memory ... just like Aaron ... The pain is so unbearable, I can't breathe and my heart feels like it's torn apart ...

⇨ *2:30 am*

I'm hearing voices telling me "Are you waiting for him to come back to help you?" Guess it's my imagination ... but somehow don't know why I feel that there's a part of me waiting for someone to come back to me. This feeling has been with me since September ... I've never told anyone about it, not even Dr. Mack. Why? I kept asking myself, and who am I waiting for? Am I starting to run away from reality again? Or am I giving up? Seriously I don't know ... what should I do? I'm too tired and no longer have the courage to recall the past ...

When I read these entries I was extremely intrigued. Who was this person that Petrina had unconsciously been waiting to come back? All evidence was pointing to Aaron. But who exactly was he? The phrase: "You are the last person I would ever hurt" seemed to come up repeatedly, and each time it appeared hurtful. Why was this so?

Also, Petrina had just produced one additional drawing in her diary – again with the same familiar key inside a wooden box within the safe. In addition, she drew a broken heart next to the key. (Fig. 10). Why did her unconscious mind bring back the image of the key repeatedly and in different forms? It had been a most fascinating experience to follow her healing journey. Intuitively, I was expecting an exciting story to unfold.

Amidst the flashbacks, the night passed.

It was 8:30 am on Thursday when Petrina woke up. She had not got much sleep the night before. After re-living her suicide attempt and re-experiencing the physical abuse from her husband she could hardly fall asleep. Nonetheless she was looking forward to her sixth therapy session.

Fig. 10: "You will be the last person that I would hurt"

She turned up promptly at 11:00 am, again alone. She looked haggard and signs of fatigue were revealing beneath her powdered face. The trauma from Joshua's violence had been most disturbing and unbearable. She quickly settled down in my consultation room and exploded into tears as she attempted to describe her emotions to me. As she cried, I took the opportunity to use the emotions of the trauma from her husband's violence as the bridge. She lapsed into a trance state rapidly.

"He beats me with his belt," she started in a desperate tone. "I could not talk. He uses masking tape on my mouth ..."

There was a pause, and she had visible difficulty continuing. She sounded helpless and her voice was tremulous. Her eyelids were flickering and her facial muscles tensed up. Her emotional tension was building up to a crescendo, and it was clear that the internal turmoil was too much for her to continue for now.

After emerging Petrina out of trance, I called for a break and let her adjourn to the washroom. On her return she looked more composed and was keen to resume the therapy. Admiring her resilience and determination, I agreed.

She regressed back to the same scene and the story picked up from where it was interrupted earlier.

"Oh ... The belt! Full of blood coming from my back. He ties me up. He likes to use the baseball bat on me. He puts it in ice and rubs the bat against my wounds."

I shuddered at the brutality.

"He starts to beat me again using the belt. I can't scream. The masking tape stops me from screaming. He places a whole packet of ice on my abdomen and waits for it to melt. After the ice melts it is painful. I can't move ... The torture lasted two weeks, every day of the week and once a day."

"What are your emotions at this point?" I held my breath as I asked.

"I am afraid ... I don't wish to wake up."

"How did you cope with it?"

"I don't know."

"What happened after the two weeks?"

"After the two weeks he went on holiday with Hazel. I pack my things and tell my mum I'm coming home. I tell my mother-in-law that I'm leaving. She says: 'I disown my son. Leave and don't ever come back.' ... I felt relieved."

"What happened after you decided to leave?"

"I lost my appetite for food. I slimmed down by ten kilograms. I am at the void deck. My friend Jessica is helping me to move house ..."

"What happened next?"

"I went home. I shut myself up for three months. I did nothing for three months ... I felt EMPTY.

"What did you do after the three months?"

"After the three months I came out and talked to a man ... I don't know who he is. I told him everything about myself. He said: 'You deserve a better man. You will forget everything.'" Again, this unidentified man sounded like Aaron.

Petrina snapped out of hypnosis at this point, looking very lost. By now, her spontaneous emergence from trance no longer surprised me. The clinic assistant, Sabiah, quickly helped her to a chair.

I sensed that Petrina had become more emotionally labile now compared to previous sessions. Sabiah served her with a cup of hot Milo while I struck up a conversation to allow her time to regain composure.

Intuitively she could read the concern on my mind. At 1:15 pm she assured me that she was feeling well enough to go home by herself. I accompanied her to the taxi stand and heaved a sigh of relief as she went off in a cab. Little did I suspect that was only the beginning of another a big dramatic event for the day.

Chapter Nine

Helplessness and Fear

*Helplessness is unquestionably the first and the surest indication
of a praying heart ... Prayer and helplessness are inseparable.
Only he who is helpless can truly pray.*
                                    – O. Hallesby

wo hours later, I received a call from Petrina. She
sounded quite helpless. I was under the assumption that
she had reached home by then, but I subsequently realized
I was wrong ...

Petrina spoke in a very frantic and pathetic tone. She said the
staff from the Human Resource Department had called her.
Someone by the name of Lorna said that HR had yet to receive
the official documentation of her hospitalization leave from her.
At the moment, she did not know what had happened to her
medical leave certificate and how to respond to HR. With her
recent lapses in memory, she was unable to recall if she had
submitted the document and to whom she had handed it to. In the
desperation of the moment she gave Lorna my mobile number
and requested her to call me.

This awkward situation came as a surprise. I had not
anticipated that her medical condition could lead to an
administrative complication. In the absence of medical
certification, Petrina's work status would be tantamount to
absence without leave and the consequences could be grave. This
was bearing in mind the hostility of her supervisor, Shirlene.

There was no doubt that the issue needed to be addressed
urgently because Lorna might call me any moment. To prevent

Petrina from getting into trouble, I needed to immediately submit a duplicate medical certificate on her behalf. This required prompt action.

I logged into the hospital computer patient record system and accessed Petrina's health records. Next, I generated a copy of her certificate of hospitalization with Dr. Shanti's name as the certifying doctor. Then I briskly walked to the Neurology Ward in search of Sister Louise. I needed her to secure Dr. Shanti's signature for me.

Luck was on my side. Sister Louise was on duty. I updated her with regards to Petrina's condition and explained to her the complexity and urgency of her situation. After that I asked her to help contact Dr. Shanti to obtain her signature.

"No problem," she said in her usual confident style. "Leave that to me. I will call you once it is done."

I went back to my office. For the first time I was beginning to feel tired and dreary. It was as if light was absent from the end of the tunnel.

Half an hour later, Sister Louise's voice was on the phone again. "Dr. Shanti has signed it and the medical certificate is ready for collection. Do you want me to send it up to you?"

Sister Louise's efficiency did not come as a surprise. She had never disappointed in her operational work since the day I first met her.

"Thanks very much, but no. I will come and collect it myself right now."

There was no time to lose. With the document in my hands, I walked right over to the HR Department. My mobile phone rang as I stepped into the lift. Lorna was on the line.

"Good afternoon, Dr. Mack. I have been instructed by my staff member, Petrina, to call you."

"Yes, I was expecting your call. In fact I am on my way up to your office right now."

"Oh!" she sounded shocked. "Okay, I will meet you at the entrance."

Up at the Human Resource Office, Lorna came out with her manager Mary to greet me. Both of them were looking rather uncomfortable at my surprise visit. I introduced myself and got straight to the point.

"I suppose this is what you want from Petrina?" I handed over the medical certificate as I talked.

"Well ... yes." Mary was searching for words to continue with the conversation. "And thank you for making a trip to our office."

I sensed that both Mary and Lorna found it difficult to understand why a senior doctor would bother to personally come to the HR Office to submit a document on a patient's behalf. After all, Petrina was only a junior clerk in the establishment.

"No problem. Is the certificate in order?"

"Oh! Yes." Mary took a quick glance at the medical certificate and continued. "I suppose with this document in place, we will be ready to process her December salary and pay her year-end bonus." Her facial tension was slowly easing off.

"Is there anything else you may need from me?" I asked.

"Well, yes ... we actually are keen to know what's happening to Petrina," Mary said. "We know she has been ill and away from work, but have no idea of her medical condition."

"Okay. Let's talk in private then."

We adjourned to a vacant interview room nearby. Lorna started the conversation. "I was the one who asked for her medical certificate because she had been away from work for quite sometime and we were not notified. She said she couldn't remember what happened to the document and that made me worried because we have heard news of her recent loss of memory. We are wondering what her status is now."

"She is on the verge of a breakdown, I am afraid," I began. There was a sign of worry on their faces.

"I am giving her therapy at the moment and hopefully she will recover by the time her medical leave expires." I paused for a moment and was deciding how much clinical information I should divulge. The two HR administrators looked concerned. They had to understand Petrina's clinical situation before they could help, I thought.

"We heard she has been unwell, hospitalized and discharged, but have no information beyond that. Now that she tells us that she cannot even remember where her things are kept, we are extremely concerned about her ability to resume work. Her supervisor had expressed the same sentiments," Mary explained.

"Well, I have not met the supervisor before," I continued, "but as far as I understand, her supervisor has triggered some of her symptoms."

Mary and Lorna were taken aback, and shot a glance at each other.

"Petrina has given me permission to talk about her problems. Her memory loss is a product of her emotional trauma, which resulted from abuse by her spouse. She has not been sleeping well for the past three years and has recently developed blackouts. She desperately needed time off from work to settle her divorce, but at the darkest moment of her life, her supervisor denied her application for one week of unpaid leave. She fainted in the Director's office, got hospitalized and has become so desperate ever since that each time the supervisor's name is mentioned, she will black out." I said it all in one breath.

"We are sorry to hear that," Mary responded apologetically. "But if she is so severely ill, do you think she will be fit to come back to work?"

"That is the very reason why we have given her one month of medical leave. She needs time to rest and recover. I can only hope that she can benefit from the therapy and recover in time. My worry is really what is going to happen when she returns to work and face the same supervisor in the same environment, after her recovery."

"Well, we actually are thinking of transferring her to the Service Quality Department on her return. Let me see if I can get the SQ Manager to arrange an interview with her when she's back."

"That would be a sound arrangement. Thank you."

I took my leave as they thanked me once again for sharing information and taking the trouble to meet them.

*****

It was 5:15 pm and I received a call from Petrina. She sounded desperate and had a nightmarish story to tell.

Apparently, for some reason, after she left the hospital in a taxi, she did not head home. Instead she ended up in a playground in Hougang Avenue 3, and could not explain how she had landed up there. She heard a lot of voices calling "Aaron" and shortly after that she blacked out.

When she regained consciousness, she was in a panic and suddenly lost all her memory. In her despair she could not even recall her home address. In a frenzy, she took out her address book and started telephoning for help. With a stroke of luck she managed to locate the number of her good friend, Bernard. Bernard, who happened to be at his computer workstation in the office, received the call and got the shock of his life. He left his office immediately, drove to the spot and found her crying desperately in a public playground. He drove her home safely.

It was obvious that she had gone to the Hougang area in search of Aaron – the individual whom she had been trying hard to identify and recall. It also became increasingly clear that Aaron had such a major influence in Petrina's life that even his name had a hold over her emotions.

Thursday, 9 December

⇨ *4:55 pm*

At around 1:50 pm, don't know why, after Dr. Mack's appointment I should be going home but somehow ended up at Hougang Ave 3 ... Can't really recall what happened ... I blackout at a playground ... before the blackout I hear lots of voices ... A man's voice he says "You can't recall Aaron, you can't take it! You must forget about him!"

I can also hear my conversation with another man. The man says "You'll be the last person that I would hurt ... Trust me I won't hurt you ..." I told him: "You said you won't hurt me! You promise not to. I trusted you, yet you've already hurt me!"

Shortly I blackout ... waking up and realize that I can't recall a single thing. Who is Aaron? What is our relationship? Seems like he has very big impact on me ... After hearing his name my memory was erased just like the computer ...When you re-install the program everything will be deleted ... My past few trips for the therapy become useless ...

Petrina reached home in a state of emotional turmoil. Intrusive-repetitive thoughts were dominating her awareness. Late that evening, she sent me a message: "I hear lots of voices with images ... I'm in confusion ... Have no idea why I keep crying. The name Aaron keeps coming up ... Who is he???"

When I subsequently had a chance to examine her diary again, it struck me that the pictures she drew that evening were consistently of a frightening nature. There was a common suicide theme in all of them.

The pictures included images of her cutting her wrist, a bottle of sleeping pills (Fig. 11), a knife and a hanging rope (Fig. 12). One of the pictures seemed to show that she was losing memory of Fabian's appearance and was trying hard to recall his identity during his funeral. From the perspective of her inner psyche, there seemed to be a widening rift between her present self in despair and the person she used to be.

Fig. 11: So many unanswered questions ...

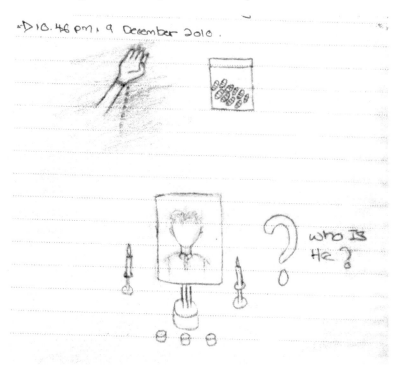

These were dark flashes of despair. Her preoccupation with the death theme frightened and worried me. As her despair deepened, what used to have meaning for her now appeared meaningless. Likewise what had been meaningless in the past seemed to be appearing meaningful.

I marveled at myself, how I had harnessed sufficient courage to go through this journey with her thus far. Yet, things were hopeful. Through these pictures she was bringing her suicidal thoughts to an open space of a shared discussion. That was a favorable sign. However, this was a difficult time. I needed to help her quench the mental agitation that was propelling her towards self-destruction. She needed an added bit of self-awareness to take a step back to obtain a fresh look at her own situation.

Thursday, 9 December
⇨ *10:46 pm*
I have these flashes of images ... whose hand was that? What has it got to do with the pills? What pill is that? And the man ... who is he? What have all these got to do with his funeral? Did he commit suicide? Have so many questions but can't find the answer ...

It was a challenge to calm a patient over the phone just as it was difficult for a person in despair to calm her own soul. Suicide had become a trapdoor that had suddenly sprung open. Her voices seemed to suggest to her that suicide was a psychological staircase (Fig. 12) that was leading her step by step to a logical culmination.

Fig. 12: "Which is your choice?"

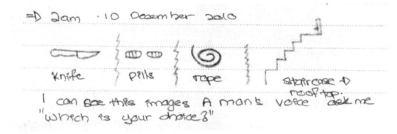

Friday, 10 December
⇨ *12:06 am*
Emptiness, Anger, Hatred, Frustration, Pain & Helplessness. I've totally lost control of my emotion ... My heart feels like as if I'm being squeezed into a very small box and tied up. Can't breathe ... I can hear

someone tell me that I don't deserve to be alive! A man's voice ...

While drawing I hear a female voice "Love and Hate?" and a very gentle female voice "Waiting to be released?" A man's voice comes in again. "He doesn't care about you, forget him! Full of empty promises! Go to bed. Tomorrow you'll forget everything." Tell me who is he? Talk to me! Why?

⇨ *4:28 am*

I feel that I start to hate myself, can't recall anything ... Why am I like that? Feels like I'm being hated as well ... I'm trapped. No matter how much I want to move. I can't ...

⇨ *7:53 am*

Slept for a few hours but the voice never leaves me ... Losing control over myself and everything. Is this the time to give up? End the journey? So tiring, so noisy ... many voices ... flashes of images ...

Fig. 13: "I don't deserve to be alive."

Petrina went through a most frightening experience on the afternoon of Friday, 10 December. She was hearing very many voices and she knew perfectly that no one else was speaking. These voices were too noisy for her to tolerate.

She asked herself: How can the voices which avow feelings alien to me and instigate abhorrent actions be part of me? Thereafter she took her antidepression medication and helped herself to sleep.

It is in our culture to regard voices as representing either mental illness or something to be feared. The fear is invariably tied up with unpredictability and the feeling of being out of control. Voices are generally regarded as a symptom of psychosis that needs to be controlled and dissipated with medication.

Here I was, trying to understand her auditory hallucinations better. By making the assumption that her voices were a form of private speech, I had taken a different perspective. This allowed her to provide a detailed account of the properties of the voices to herself and be better able to manage her own fear. Equally important was my reminder to her about the benefit of the discreet and timely use of medication in controlling her symptoms as and when the need arose.

Fig. 14: "Empty Promise"

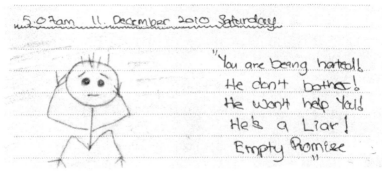

Petrina woke up at 6:40 pm that evening and the voices had temporarily stopped haunting her. She felt better and was calmer.

She knew she had been through a lot of stress lately and was not keen to become dependent on the antipsychotic medication to manage her voices.

Saturday, 11 December
⇨ *6:49 am*

I took the medicine again. The voices are coming back ... whose voice was it? What does it mean? I'm tired already ...

⇨ *1:57 pm*

The moment I stop taking medicine it comes back again. Have no choice, but to take the medicine again ...

⇨ *10:13 pm*

Just wake up ... I'm looking back at my journal, didn't realize that I've been through so much ... feels like I'm leading a double life as if all that's happened was not me ... can't recall anything ... can only recall bits and pieces ... My mind is like a piece of blank paper ... wonder how I pull through all these ...

When I subsequently got to read her journal entries, the description of her feelings and loss of autobiographical memory sounded very much like that of a dissociated identity. She seemed to have a disruption in the integrative functions of consciousness and perception of the environment. All these were signs of severe emotional trauma and the development of intrapsychic conflict.

Sunday, *12 December*
⇨ *10:00 pm*

Maybe forgetting all the unhappy memories is a good thing ... Provided it doesn't lead to any health issue. Guess it's time for me to really face the reality and move on be it I like it or not! Just don't wish to be a burden to my family.

That night I interacted with Nurse Beatrice via email. She commented that Petrina's story sounded "like a drama, but it won't be pleasant to be part of it".

She wrote: "At 25 years of age, her life is all messed up. If she goes back to work, she will be affected by the gossips and her condition will get worse again. It is going to be a long journey for her." I resonated with her comments.

Petrina had a very turbulent weekend and her desire to recall the memory of Aaron was overwhelming. By then she had been taking her antidepressants thrice daily and she felt rather drowsy. However, it had been a very long time since she'd had a good sleep and peaceful feeling, and so for the moment, she didn't mind the side effects of the medication.

She finally asked me for a favor. She had come to the undeniable conclusion that knowledge of Aaron's identity was crucial to her recovery process. However, as she did not have the courage to call Aaron herself, she asked me to do it on her behalf.

I hesitated. Would it be appropriate for me to do so? Would I be perceived as intruding into others' privacy? However, in the interest of Petrina's health, I dialed Aaron's number.

The phone rang twice. Aaron promptly answered my call. I was delighted. I introduced myself as the doctor looking after Petrina's illness and explained the purpose of my call. He answered politely and confirmed that he did know Petrina in person. I then elaborated on Petrina's health status and explained why she needed help urgently from him.

There was a moment of silence from Aaron. I sensed reluctance. His tone struck me as lacking the kind of concern that would be expected from someone who had been so close to Petrina and who had earlier volunteered to help her out of her depression. I did not give up. I conveyed Petrina's plea for help and highlighted the importance of recovering her memory. I asked if he would mind giving her a call or meeting up with me in my clinic at some convenient time. He deliberated over his reply and the ultimate response was an ambiguous one.

Eventually I had to contact Aaron a second time. Petrina had a suggestion. She wanted to meet him in my clinic on her next appointment on Monday, 13 December. To this request, Aaron declined. He replied categorically that he was unable to commit. No reason was given.

I felt stuck with the situation …

Chapter Ten

Struggle to Recall

Whatever the struggle, continue the climb. It may be only one step to the summit.

– Diane Westlake

Over the weekend, Petrina had sent me a worrisome SMS message:

"Hi. Dr. Mack, I've been taking the antidepression medicine because I've been hearing too much voices, very noisy ... Almost go along with the voice to cut myself with the penknife"

I empathized with her, and for a moment I was at a loss for how to respond. After some deliberation, I told her the truth. In part I thought it was important for her to know about Aaron's reluctance to help, and in part I also wanted to see if she was strong enough to face up to the reality of her relationship with that man.

"Okay, I guess that Aaron did something that hurt me. That's why he dare not face me ..." she replied calmly. "Doesn't matter. I have confidence that I can get over him." She responded in a matter-of-fact tone.

I felt a little relieved. At the same time, I promised her that I would explore the option of assisting her in regaining her memory directly through hypnotherapy. Hopefully I could succeed.

*****

On Monday, 13 December, Petrina came to my clinic, again alone. This would be her seventh therapy session. Again she appeared all ready and set for it.

By now she had experienced the hypnotic state many times, and connecting her with her subconscious mind was a straightforward task. She sank into a deep trance quickly and I decided to use the filing-cabinet metaphor in my hypnotic script. This is a metaphor innovated by Roger Allen in his book *Scripts and Strategies in Hypnotherapy*. The metaphor is the basis of a visual imagery used to help patients access their forgotten memories and evaluate their own repression.

"You will recall that I have told you that all your past memories in your life are stored in your unconscious mind like a filing cabinet ..." I started by priming her with a suggestion.

"And now your subconscious mind will assist you to go through that filing cabinet, to uncover those memories of importance to you ... especially those memories that relate to your problems of blackouts and of recall of Aaron's identity ..." I put more suggestions into her mind.

"As you relax and go deeper, I will count from one to three ... and as I reach the count of three you will see that you are reaching out to open a door and enter a room where the filing cabinet is placed."

As this was a long hypnotic script, I made use of her ideomotor response to confirm that she was indeed visualizing the imagery that I suggested.

"You are now inside the room and see a table in the center. To the side of the table is a tall filing cabinet with four gray drawers and one black drawer at the bottom. The gray drawers contain all the day-to-day memories of your life and will be available to you anytime you need," I continued.

"The black drawer contains memories that your unconscious mind has decided to keep away from you. The answers to the problems that you have been facing with Aaron are all in this black drawer. Within this black drawer are those memories that are the basis of your misery. Once revealed to your conscious awareness they cannot cause you problems anymore."

I paused for a moment, and resumed. "As the black drawer slides open, you will see a number of files inside it. Tell me, Petrina, how many files are there inside?"

"There are four," she replied softly but promptly.

"Good. Now, as your unconscious mind is taking out the first file from the drawer and putting it on the table, you open and look at it … Tell me what you see."

"I am waiting for Mum to come back. I am lonely …" she started.

The word "lonely" immediately struck me as significant. As she went on to describe her fearful feelings of being alone I listened intently. I believed I could understand that she had previously done all she could to avoid being alone. This included her clinging on to a destructive relationship. Hence she ended up in her current state. Now that she had bared her emotions, I asked her to go to the end of the last page of the file and put it on the table.

"Now open up the second file and tell me what is inside it."

"Joshua betrayed me. Lots of empty promises. He says when we get married he will give me a custom wedding ... All his bills not settled … Hatred … I used to love him a lot … Hazel … she betrayed me. Joshua … he abused me."

Petrina was getting emotional. Again I could understand how painful it could be for her to acknowledge that someone whom she loved and whom she believed had also loved her could actually be abusing her physically. She had been making excuses for his behavior and wanted to give him the benefit of the doubt.

I next told her to close the second file and open the third one.

Petrina then described her negative experience with her emotionally abusive supervisor. Shirlene appeared to be the sort of person who had an excessive need to exert control over others.

"Shirlene ... I begged her for leave. She said it is me who is harping on my unhappy past. I am very tired. She forced me to work. I begged her for unpaid leave. I wanted to see the doctor. But she says she would not help me. I feel very pathetic. She put all the pains on me. She says: 'You will lose your job if you continue like that.'"

"Now that you have reached the end of your third file, I want you to leave that file on the table and open up the fourth file. What do you find inside?" I had been waiting eagerly to hear what hidden memories would emerge and if Aaron's name would come up.

There was a pause. "I see Fabian and Aaron ..." she said. Bingo! I was expecting her to elaborate on Aaron.

"I hear voices ..." she continued. "It's no good for you." She paused again, struggling, as if she was in agony. Suddenly she said "I can't recall!" and opened her eyes.

Ever since she started therapy, this was the sixth time Petrina had snapped out of hypnosis at the mention of Aaron.

She became wide awake, stared at the ceiling for a moment and got up from the couch, looking depressed and somewhat apologetic. The session had not turned out to my expectation. Without a word, she reached out to her handbag and took out a cinema ticket. I looked at it and saw the words "Golden Village Cinema". The ticket was an old one dated 5 July 2010.

"As I told you the last time, the fifth of July is a date that I felt very strongly attached to, and I do not know why." She talked in a pitiful voice.

I stared at her intently and asked, "Was it a special movie?"

"I simply cannot recall what movie we watched, nor with whom I went." She looked at me earnestly.

"Was it with Aaron?"

"I don't know. I just cannot remember. Do you think you can help me?"

Through the window of her eye I sensed how desperate she was. I was facing a problem of memory repression. Worse still, the memory repression was being used by a patient as a psychological defense mechanism against emotional pain. For a while I wondered what to say. I was not sure where the mystery underlying her repressed memory was leading us to. Yet, from the technical viewpoint, it should not be difficult to resolve that issue using the hypnotic technique.

We agreed on another attempt.

Petrina returned to the couch and repositioned herself. She quickly entered a trance state and I regressed her awareness back to that important moment on the fifth day of July.

"You are now back to the 5 July 2010 and you see yourself at the Golden Village Cinema ... Now tell me what is happening."

"Oh, I am now at the cinema in Tampines Mall. It is dark inside the cinema. The movie had started ... I am together with a man watching the movie *Karate Kid*."

"Who exactly is this man whom you are with?"

"He is a tall, tanned-looking person ..." she said slowly and still deep in trance. Then her eyebrows started to furrow. "Oh! I'll tell you who he is ..." she suddenly exclaimed. In a moment of truth she blurted out: "He is Aaron."

Although she sounded excited over her discovery, this really was an expected finding for me. All clues so far had been pointing to the identity of this key person as being Aaron. However, it was heartening to see her face lighting up, even though she was in trance. It sounded like a Eureka moment for her, and I felt happy.

At this point something unusual seemed to be happening. Petrina was still in trance. I suddenly heard a mix of unidentified noises and there were signs that she was feeling internally agitated. She started to sound confused and unable to recall any further. As our objective had been achieved I thought it was time to emerge her from her trance state.

In my usual manner of reversing a patient from hypnosis, I started counting backwards from five to one. Something most fascinating happened. Upon reaching the count of one, she did not emerge. Instead she remained deeply in trance. I waited a while but she showed no signs of lightening her trance state. I was about to try emerging her a second time when I suddenly heard a couple of different voices coming out from her throat. It sounded as if someone was trying to start a conversation inside her.

Next moment, I realized that the "parts" inside her were talking. They were the same parts that I had previously called out during the therapy session on 2 December. These parts had now emerged spontaneously from the depths of her inner psyche. Furthermore they were posing as different personae and started a dialogue on their own!

It was awesome.

The same two parts, LOST and HAPPY, whose respective roles were to prevent memory recall and make Petrina happy, had appeared. They were actively talking and quibbling in the background.

This was an unexpected development and I had to think on my feet. I abandoned my original attempt to bring her out of trance, and instead decided to flow with her self-induced parts-therapy.

Dr. Mack: Who am I speaking to, please?
LOST: It's Lost.
Dr. Mack: Why did you suddenly appear?
LOST: I will not let Petrina recall. [meaning about Aaron]
Dr. Mack: Why not?
LOST: It is not good for her.
Dr. Mack: What do you think, Happy? Should Petrina recall Aaron's identity?

HAPPY: [Avoiding the issue] Aaron is a kind man. He is stuck between the family and Petrina.

Dr. Mack: Is it best for Petrina to forget him then?

HAPPY: For the time being, yes.

Dr. Mack: But she is not happy until she recovers her memory of him.

LOST: Petrina should confront Aaron, but not now.

HAPPY: I agree with Lost that Petrina should confront Aaron, but only when the correct time comes.

Dr. Mack: How long should Petrina wait before doing so?

HAPPY: I don't know. Aaron hurts Petrina and does not know he has hurt her. Petrina does not like it and threatens to kill herself.

LOST: Aaron triggers all of Petrina's loss of memory. They shouldn't talk to each other. He has to be responsible. He knows what she went through and he has hurt her. She will have to confront Aaron one day, but only when the time is correct.

Dr. Mack: Petrina, are you agreeable to that?

Petrina: [emphatically] The *key* is with Aaron. It is the *key* to Petrina's heart.

Dr. Mack: Happy, how do you think you can help Petrina to remember Aaron?

HAPPY: Lost is blocking.

LOST: Petrina will forget Aaron. The trauma from Joshua is too great. She cannot take another one. Aaron is the *key* person as to why she cannot remember things.

Dr. Mack: What exactly is Aaron's relationship with Petrina?

LOST: I won't tell. It's all empty promises.

Dr. Mack:	By empty promises, who are you referring to, Joshua or Aaron?
LOST:	Both of them.
Dr. Mack:	Does Aaron love Petrina at all?
LOST:	I don't know.
Dr. Mack:	How to help Petrina then?
LOST:	Well ... confront Aaron. Let him know that he made her suffer ... but now is not the time.
Dr. Mack:	Is there a better way?
LOST:	She has lost her memory. She loves Aaron. She will only remember Joshua and Shirlene now because I've blocked her memory of Aaron.
Dr. Mack:	Happy, what do you suggest?
HAPPY:	Petrina does not want to forget.
Petrina:	Forgetting won't help because the *key* is with Aaron.
HAPPY:	I agree with Lost that Petrina should confront Aaron at some time.
Dr. Mack:	Petrina, do you agree with that?
Petrina:	Okay. I agree with everyone to leave Aaron aside now and confront him when the suitable time comes.

The outcome of the discussion with the parts did not seem to add much in terms of finding a solution or providing new insights. Interestingly I noticed the repeated reference to the *key* that was with Aaron. I couldn't understand its symbolic significance at this point in time. It remained a puzzle as to why Petrina's inner psyche was resisting the recall of Aaron's identity. The consensus of the parts were to confront Aaron only when the time was "suitable" without any indication of when this might be. I felt that I was none the wiser.

I took a break while Petrina went to the washroom. I needed time to think through a new approach to breaking the deadlock.

While waiting for her, the therapeutic approach taken by the famous hypnotherapist Dr. Edith Fiore came to my mind. She had helped her patients with all sorts of clinical problems with her methods. She always explored first for a cause in the patient's present life and when she couldn't find one, she would search the patient's past lives. Very often, at the root of these problems was a past life story that was responsible for the patient's present life symptoms.

The theory behind this approach is karmic and based on the principle of cause and effect. Any cause that has not produced its effect yet is regarded as an event that is awaiting completion. This creates an imbalance in energy in the process and the balancing of energy may not occur within the span of a single lifetime. If the energy imbalance needs to right itself in another lifetime, individuals need insight and knowledge of their souls and reincarnation to understand the meaning of the events of their current life and the effects of their own responses to them.

Petrina returned from the washroom. Remembering that she was of Buddhist faith, and had no religious conflict with the reincarnation concept, I suggested the option of a past life therapy. She agreed promptly.

As this was her first past life regression I chose a hypnotic induction. Once down in a trance state, Petrina regressed back to a past life in China, and a story set in the scene of the Qing Dynasty rapidly emerged.

Petrina was an imperial concubine in her past life and she was the favorite concubine of the Emperor, whom she described as "tall and tanned-looking". There were palace politics and she was having serious conflicts with the Empress. Then the past life story started to flow.

"I am getting married. I am being married to the Emperor," she whispered.

"Tell me more," I prompted.

"Someone tied me up. I am inside a well. The Emperor saves me. He brings me back to his room. He gives me medication. The medicine is bitter. I'm sleeping …" The story was gaining suspense.

The past life scene progressed. "The Emperor starts to like me … I killed the Empress and I become the Empress myself. After that I have nightmares every night. I dream of myself killing the Empress. In the end I killed myself."

Apparently, as the story went, the Empress was a wicked person. She had been mistreating people and tortured all the other imperial concubines. The Emperor didn't like her and Petrina, as his favorite concubine, strongly felt that she was morally right in getting rid of her. Of course, there was a price to pay. At her funeral, the Emperor and many people were weeping.

I then decided to obtain more detailed information about her murder plot for the Empress.

"Go back to the point when you killed the Empress."

"I have instructed the chef to poison the Empress. It is a deadly dosage, given daily for one month in the food. She died after one month. She has no idea that I killed her."

"What happened after she died?"

"I have nightmares. I see the Empress dying with her eyes open." A sense of chill went through my shoulders.

"What are your emotions at this stage?"

"Afraid."

"What thought goes with your emotion of being afraid?"

"My hands are full of blood … but it is worth it. By killing her, I saved a lot of other people."

"What happened after that?"

"I continued to have the nightmares for seven years. I feel afraid, but I've done the right thing." There seemed to be no sense of remorse.

"Go to the point where you killed yourself."

"I am sick. I have heart problem. I hanged myself. I don't want the Emperor to see me suffering."

"How did you feel at this point?"

"Suffocated," she said. The word seemed to have struck a chord. It sounded very familiar.

"What thoughts go with the feeling of suffocation?"

"Very scary … It will soon be over …" Petrina snapped out of hypnosis with a strange look on her face. I was a little puzzled and somewhat disappointed.

My initial thought was that the past life story seemed to have little relevance to her problem at hand. What struck me was the feeling of suffocation that she described just before she emerged. The sense of being "suffocated" was something that she had repeatedly been experiencing in her recent illness during her earlier therapy sessions. She had also expressed that explicitly in her journal writing and her vivid hand drawings. What made her so scared at the last part of the regression was something I could not ascertain.

It was a pity that I did not have a chance to explore her death scene in greater detail. As a rule in past life therapy, the moment of death is the point where most of the healing occurs. What she described sounded like a sad, traumatic death and the grief felt by her dying soul would likely be for her lover the Emperor who had been left behind. I would expect all her unresolved thoughts and feelings surrounding the moment of death to coalesce and form a highly charged imprint on her soul memory, the essence of which would have been transferred to the current lifetime.

Of note, Petrina was unusually quiet after the past life regression. That made me uncomfortable. After the session, she did not comment on her own past life story at all, and instead looked a little perplexed. For a moment, I guessed she was feeling like I did, somewhat disappointed that the story had not added value in recalling Aaron's identity.

I pondered over the situation and after some minutes I thought I would do something differently to diffuse her anxiety.

One week ago, another of my hypnotherapy patients had just returned from a mission trip from Thailand. On her way home she passed by a music shop in Bangkok and chanced upon a set of music CDs called "Meditation – Green Music". Identifying the melodies as something that I would love, she purchased them and gave them to me as an early Christmas gift. I had kept the CDs in my office since.

The CDs were produced by Chamras Saewataporn and I had enjoyed listening to the entire series on the very day I received them. Each disk contained an hour-long musical piece of soulful music that would guide the listener to an inner sense of serenity. Of the three, I picked up the one that was entitled: "A Journey to Inner Peace". It carried an inspiring message tagline: *The walk is never-ending. The path is exhausting. Yet the destination is truly self-rewarding.* The message resonated very closely with my own emotions.

I have always felt that music has the unique power to bring us to an awareness of our feelings in an unfettered way. Meditation music in particular had been serving as a stimulus to assist me in my own descent into my unconscious mind. I got my office secretary to burn a copy and passed it to Petrina. I assured her that she would definitely find it useful.

*****

I went home that evening feeling mentally tired. My spirits were lower than usual. The outcome of my therapy efforts had not lived up to my own expectations and I had still been unable to figure out the mystery behind Petrina's illness. I had failed to understand why she had not been recovering the way that she should after all the efforts I had put in.

Perhaps everything in life happened for a specific reason, I told myself. I shifted my mind off work and took a little walk in the garden by the poolside. The evening breeze was soothing and gently dispelled my emotional burden. The scent of flowers and garden shrubs was enlivening and suddenly I felt connected with nature again.

At about 6:30 pm, while my wife was preparing dinner, I relaxed on my home sofa, opened my laptop computer and logged on to Facebook. As I looked through the new posts appearing on my Facebook page, someone suddenly attracted my attention. The profile picture of a familiar face appeared under the "friends-on-chat" column. It was Eileen!

Eileen was another unusual patient of mine I had not met for some time and suddenly an idea came to my mind. I decided to make good use of the Facebook chat function.

I clicked on Eileen's profile picture, and a chat box shot up from the bottom right-hand corner of the computer screen. "Good evening!" I typed.

"Hi, Dr. Mack. How are things with you?" Her response was prompt.

Eileen was a Eurasian lady and had been a patient of mine for many years. She had developed an incisional hernia after a previous Caesarian section. Some years ago she was suffering from recurrent pain from the hernia and was referred to me by her gynecologist. After some procrastination, I operated on her and she had an uneventful recovery. Over the course of time, as I got to know her better, she confided in me that she had clairvoyant abilities from young. After growing up she advanced in her psychic development. As a child she had been regarded by her parents as bringing bad luck to the family because of her unearthly visions. She was of Catholic upbringing, and loved talking to her angels. As she grew up she met a parish priest one day and was taught how to put her natural psychic gifts to good use. Since then she had come to terms with her extrasensory ability and had been helping others through her psychic consciousness. She had however remained humble, friendly and loving, and we had stayed in touch ever since.

"Hi, Eileen. I think I need your advice with regards to a patient problem of mine," I typed cautiously.

"Oh, I have been waiting for your call for the past few days. You finally contacted me today."

It was a most astonishing response!

For several seconds, I was dumbfounded. How could she have known my problem? What was going on? The adrenaline level in my bloodstream instantly shot up. My heart was thumping hard. I took a deep breath, and laughed to myself while shaking my head in disbelief! Was I dreaming?

Then I calmed down, reminding myself that I was now interacting with a psychically developed individual who had proven extrasensory capabilities.

"You mean, you have actually been anticipating my call?!" I asked, controlling my excitement.

"Yes," she replied coolly.

"I'm surprised!" I couldn't help exclaiming.

"I sensed that you are having a problem and expected you to be calling me for help any moment. I have been waiting all this while."

"Oh, I see!" My fingers trembled a little as I fumbled over the computer keyboard. I took another deep breath before starting to type ferociously.

"Yes, this patient of mine is a 25-year-old lady who has been badly abused by her ex-husband. She went through three abortions and developed guilt feelings and depression. She has suffered severe emotional trauma with selective memory loss and is now experiencing sudden blackouts repeatedly. I have given her several sessions of hypnotherapy. Although overall she has improved, her blackouts and memory loss have again been triggered by a 'voice' that she heard while she was on her way home in a taxi. She ended up not going home but somewhere else in a playground in Hougang. She could not remember what happened and why she went there. Worse still, she temporarily forgot where her home address was at the moment and cried in desperation. In the end, she got help from a friend and reached home. She and her mum were freaked out. All her clinical improvement from her therapy seemed to have gone down the drain."

I typed out the problem all in a single action. Then I paused and continued typing again.

"She came again today for therapy and I continue to do what I can to help her to regain her inner peace. I do not want to give up. However, I am beginning to wonder if I am the correct person and really have the ability to help her out of her predicament. Can you help to give me some advice on this situation?"

This was the first time I had sought help of this nature from Eileen, but I never doubted her willingness to assist. My experience with her was that no matter whom I talked about, she would be able to visualize the person's appearance and somehow know who I was referring to. She had shared with me her wonderful ability to be able to quickly access a mental image of the individual in question with just a short prayer followed by a brief meditation. Images of individuals obtained in this manner were usually not of full body size, but sufficiently clear to be able to take action on.

It took a little while before Eileen replied. Again, her response amazed me.

"This poor soul is trying her best to come out of the darkest hole that she is in. Please don't give up on her. The charm that the husband used is of Thai origin."

I was shocked at the reply!

What had happened? What was this charm all about? I had never heard of Petrina mentioning any religious worship of Thai origin, nor of any magical practices that her husband could be involved in. However, I knew Eileen as a person whose words I would never doubt.

"You mean she's under some kind of a spell?" I reworded her message carefully to be really sure I understood her fully.

"In my mind I see lots of Thai figurines in a dark room," she wrote.

"Oh dear!" I was in dismay. "To my knowledge, Thai charms are very difficult to handle. I have no experience in dealing with them. How should I approach this problem?"

"Do not worry. You will be able to help her. All is not lost yet. She came to you at the right time."

I was feeling a little troubled by this new revelation. "I am feeling very inadequate myself ... and if I do not persist, this poor girl is not going to recover. How am I going to handle this?"

"My prayer group is on the high alert and are all very prayerful right now. Poor lady ... she has been through so much. We must try and help her," she continued.

"Grateful for your offer to help. God will bless you," I wrote.

"God's blessing be always upon you and you will be guided and protected. We will do our best for this lady with God's blessing."

I logged off Facebook, feeling a little confused and uncertain. My mind was in a whirl. I discussed the issue with my wife at dinner time. She reassured me that I would be able to overcome the obstacle. Anyway, she knew I would never consider turning back as an option at this stage.

I went to bed that night with an unanswered question. Had Petrina been under a spell all along?

Chapter Eleven
Meeting the Challenge

What would life be if we had no courage to attempt anything?
– Vincent van Gogh

I t so happened that at the very same time as I was engaged on a Facebook chat with Eileen, Petrina was having a little quiet, reflective time to herself.

Although she had been taciturn and reserved in expression after today's therapy, she had in fact, unknown to me, experienced a substantial clinical improvement. In fact by now she had recovered a major portion, if not most of her memory. For some reason, she did not divulge that immediately after the therapy session. What remained to be resolved was only the "mystery" behind her relationship with Aaron.

She was at home listening to the meditation CD quietly by herself that evening. She had been using artwork to gain spiritual serenity and now she was trying to experience the same through music. There was a sense of calmness and peace that she had not felt before. With the impact of mindfulness meditation, the strife and discord that had been overwhelming her in the recent week was now peeling off from her like layers of onion skin.

Later that evening, a little elated, she wrote in her journal:

Monday, 13 December
⇨ 8:20 pm
After today's therapy I have recalled most of the memory. It's a good sign ☺. The only thing is Aaron. I'm afraid of him but have to face it. I could recall some of my

colleagues, my friends, my ex-husband, most of what I went through after listening to the meditation disc Dr. Mack burned for me ... Guess will recover very soon ☺ !

The meditative state lasted about three hours and she was drifting into a hypnagogic state by 11:00 pm. Unfortunately trouble was brewing again.

Voices had started to return. Audible conversations were keeping her awake. It seemed like the "guilt" part of her was talking. Petrina later recalled that she was quite certain that she heard her own voice saying: "Your life is very miserable, you should not be alive."

At one stage Petrina heard a voice telling her to end her life by cutting her wrist. In a transitional state between wakefulness and sleep she went along with the instructions of the voice. She took a penknife in her right hand and slowly made a 3 cm transverse cut over the palmar aspect of her left wrist. Soon, the pain of the incision brought her back into the conscious state.

She suddenly gained consciousness. Shocked at her foolishness, she asked herself: What am I doing? Quickly dropping the knife, she examined her wrist. She was blessed. The skin laceration was superficial and had spared the vessels lying in the deeper layer. The bleeding was minimal and she was safe. She cleaned and dressed the wound and tried going back to sleep.

It was a very tough moment. For the past two weeks Petrina had made a determined effort to get well and she had already gone a long way. She reaffirmed to herself again that she would not waste her efforts and would stay strong and recover quickly. That night, she resorted to taking the anti-anxiety medication again to calm herself. She reminded herself that she needed to keep going.

⇨ *11:25 pm*

I can't go on like that. I have to confront Aaron tomorrow ... I don't have much time left. I want to recover ... What exactly happened between us? Why is it that he is unwilling to help? Just hope tomorrow I'll be able to help him ...! Just wish to get over him!

The medication helped, and she managed to fall asleep after a while, but only to be awakened again in the early hours of the morning by further voices. This time the voices sounded very much like that of Aaron.

Tuesday, 14 December
⇨ *3:09 am*

I hear conversation like "I miss you", and "Petrina, confront him; it's time now" ... Was it my imagination? I don't know ...

Deep down was a strong urge to confront Aaron once and for all and she reckoned that the time had now come for her to proceed. She said to herself: "No, I have to get things done immediately. When the morning comes I have to go to Aaron's house or his company office to confront him."

It was a terrible struggle to fall asleep that night. Petrina got up in the morning and was fully determined that she would get to the bottom of the matter. Her parents and her brothers had all gone to work and she decided that she would handle the matter alone. In the event that Aaron was not willing to help her recover her memory, she would be psychologically prepared to get over the emotional hardship all by herself. She told herself she couldn't afford to delay her recovery any further. It was time to take the plunge even if she had to confront Aaron single-handedly …

Forgetting all the unhappy memories is a good thing ...
Provided it doesn't lead to any health issue. Guess it's
time for me to really face the reality and move on be it I
like it or not. I just don't want to be a burden to my
family.

It was 9:00 am on the morning of 14 December. Petrina looked up Aaron's telephone number and company address. The taxi drove her to a place in Hougang. It was a residential area, to her surprise.

On her way there, she kept asking herself: Should I or should I not do this? Is it better to let all my unhappy memories stay forgotten? However, an inner force was pushing her on. She knew she had to heal herself and needed to move fast.

On arrival, she found herself within a block of residential HDB (Housing Development Board) flats that were built under the government's public housing subsidy scheme. The area was sited near to the junction between Hougang Avenue and Upper Serangoon Road. Several blocks in the area had been recently re-painted with blue and yellow colors. There were no signs of any shop houses or commercial units.

She took a lift up to level six and was surprised to find that there was no signboard to indicate the presence of a business office. If anything, it looked every inch a residential unit. Eventually she found out that Aaron had doubled up his residential premises as his business office.

She hesitated for several moments and did not have the courage to press the door bell. After some deliberation, she called Aaron's number as shown in her address phone book. Someone picked up the phone and she asked: "Is there such a person called Aaron?"

"Ya, there is," Aaron replied, "and you are ...?"

"I am Miss Teh," she introduced herself meekly. "I need a favor from you. I am standing just outside the entrance to your apartment. Can I talk to you face to face?" Silence followed, and the phone line was disconnected.

Thirty seconds passed. The door opened. A young, tall and tanned-looking man appeared. He had dark, thick eyebrows and short, straight hair that was uncombed and fluffy and with a parting to the right of the midline. He kept a long sideburn. His eyes were dark and a little piercing in his gaze.

In front of her stood the man who had plagued her life for the past three months. He was the one who had repeatedly triggered her emotional crises, showered her with nightmares and haunted her with auditory hallucinations. She had suffered multiple syncopal attacks because of him. Yet, he remained a stranger to her at this moment in time. Petrina was totally unable to recognize him!

They stared at each other for a moment. Her heart sank and hesitated over what to say next. Aaron continued to look at her calmly and behaved as if he had never known her before.

After a few moments Petrina's attention was diverted by his physical appearance, especially his tanned complexion. She broke the ice and asked: "Are you a local?"

"Don't I look like a local?" he responded dryly, still showing no sign of inviting her into the house.

"No. You just don't look like a local to me, or are you?" she asked curiously. "But your surname is Yeong, right?"

"Hmm." He nodded his head.

As she continued to scrutinize him visually for clues, she was struggling in her mind trying to remember how she could be related to or connected with this "stranger" in front of her. Her mind was turning a little heavy and muddled. Bits and pieces of memories were fighting to filter through, and the jigsaw puzzles were scrambling to search for a fit. She experienced a few immediate flashbacks, but making sense out of the available pieces of scanty information was no easy task at this stressful moment.

She continued to work hard to focus herself mentally. Anxiety was mounting. A fear of the unknown was overwhelming her. Next, a frightening chill went right through her whole body. She felt as if she was standing on forbidden ground, or had trespassed some sacred boundaries. Her body started to shiver but she couldn't understand why. It was 9:30 am on a sunny Tuesday morning and the air temperature was lukewarm. Yet the fine oscillations of the muscles of the extremities were rapidly increasing in both frequency and amplitude to the extent that they were visible as coarse tremors.

"My name is Petrina ..." she introduced herself with a trembling voice. By now she felt much pressure within, especially with the complicated task of explaining the purpose of her visit. There was too much uncertainty with the "stranger" standing in front of her, made worse by her fear of not knowing what to expect from this man in terms of his reaction and helpfulness.

"Yes, Petrina, how can I help?" He continued to talk in an expressionless manner. Petrina was tongue-tied for a moment.

"You look as if you are feeling very cold," Aaron added, but showed no signs of making an effort to invite her into his house.

After getting over her shivering, she gathered enough courage to explain that she was currently suffering from memory loss and believed he was the correct person to help her to recover. Aaron had stayed sober all this while. He implicitly agreed to help her. However, instead of inviting her into his house, he took her down to the void deck to continue with their conversation.

A very challenging dialogue began. As the content to be elicited from this conversation was going to be critical for her recovery of her memory, Petrina asked Aaron for permission to use a voice recorder. However, he categorically refused, saying that he wasn't comfortable with the idea. Instead, he allowed her to take down written notes only.

She took out her pen and diary from her handbag, and opened the book to the page of her last entry. She began to craft her questions mentally, and the beginning of a complex and painful process of memory recall had just begun ...

Aaron was a polytechnic graduate in 2001, majoring in Electronics and Communications Engineering. He subsequently went for his degree program in Psychology at Murdoch University and graduated in 2009. Petrina had always considered him a "psychologist" and admired him as such. Upon graduation, he joined a management company called PEACE Consulting Services that provided management training for organizational and human capital development.

Petrina remembered that she had first met Aaron within the hospital campus when he came to facilitate the induction course for new employees organized by the Service Quality Department. That was held in March 2010. Although she had taken up employment in September 2009, the staff shortage did not allow her to come for induction until six months later.

There were 18 employees attending that induction. Although meeting for the first time, Petrina and Aaron experienced an unexplainable feeling of being connected with each other. It was a feeling of familiarity as if they had already known each other for a long time. In the course of the training, Aaron had been noticed by the other participants to be frequently looking in Petrina's direction for long uninterrupted moments. On Petrina's part she had found the course boring. Her mind was preoccupied with her divorce proceedings and she wasn't in a mood to listen to the management talk. What struck her subsequently as remarkable was the fact that she kept experiencing visions of a key in her unconscious mind throughout the session while Aaron was talking. It was as if she had seen the key being worn around someone's neck. Furthermore it appeared to be the same key she had drawn in her diary twice ...

"Aaron actually approached me personally and asked me how long I had been employed. I told him about six months. When he was communicating with me I actually had flashes of images of the key, but never really bothered to take note of it," Petrina recalled.

Fig. 15: "The Key is with Aaron."

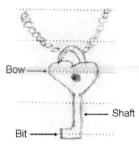

Intriguingly, ever since that day of the induction course she continued to perceive flashes of the image of the key off and on for the next four months until her first date with Aaron in July 2010. There was something very consistent with the shape, appearance and make-up of the key, regardless of whether the image appeared in her vision, drawings or dreams. It was a golden key with a red ruby at the center of the heart-shaped bow with a short shaft and a flat rectangular bit (Fig. 15). There was also a semicircular ring attached to the bow with a chain of pearls going through the ring.

The date when they first went out together was 5 July 2010. At that time Aaron was quite sweet to her. After watching a movie that evening they ate sashimi for dinner in a Japanese restaurant. Since then they had been going out every Saturday evening.

At that time Petrina started to ask herself whether she should or shouldn't allow their relationship to progress and develop further. She had only just started divorce proceedings two months before and was barely getting over the trauma of her abusive husband. Intuitively, she felt that a hurried commitment to a new relationship soon after breaking off from an abusive one was not a wise move. On the other hand, she needed company. Her original circle of friends that were close to Hazel and Joshua had all left her and she felt lonely.

Aaron seemed to have good listening skills and showed empathy. Yet Petrina repeatedly rejected the idea of entering a new relationship initially. Then Aaron put it to her in a different tone: "It is up to you whether you want to let go and move on. I reach out my hand to you and it is your choice as to whether you want to take it or not. My family is very open-minded. They don't mind our relationship."

Aaron was very confident that their relationship would eventually work out. One of the reasons he quoted was that his own mother was a divorcee and could appreciate the feelings behind someone who had a failed marriage. The chances of his mother objecting to him establishing a relationship with a divorced woman would therefore be low.

Petrina felt very tempted to accept his offer but continued to be hesitant for a while. She had just gotten over the nightmare of facing an abusive husband and the fear of another failure was prohibitive. On the other hand, she was hoping that her healing process could be accelerated if she could find a mental anchor in another trusted person.

Up to this point in her life, she knew she had not had a chance to discover herself. She had been trying to be what others had expected her to be. She had accepted what others had been telling her about who she was and what her motivations in life were. Now she needed a change. She needed an opportunity to discover her own nature and start life all over again. At this stage she was drawn towards the temptation of being supported by and dependent on a male partner to make the next part of her life a success.

Eventually, on 11 August Petrina and Aaron decided to go steady with each other. This was a date that Petrina held closely to her heart. Their relationship heated up soon afterwards, to the extent that he would send her SMS messages every hour. Despite the fact that she put a lot of effort into the relationship, she was conscious of the fact that she had barely two months of contact time with him and might not know him in depth. By the time she became emotionally committed she found it increasingly difficult to be objective in her assessment of his personality and her own situation.

"I have gone through a lot in my previous marriage, and I really don't want to go through the same thing again in our relationship," she told Aaron once, feeling somewhat insecure.

"You will be the last person I will ever hurt ..." was the reassuring statement from Aaron.

Unfortunately things did not turn out the way Aaron promised. He failed repeatedly to turn up for appointments with her. After that, he stopped answering her phone calls and remained uncontactable for days. When confronted, he would give the same excuse every time that he had been busy. Eventually she was told that his parents objected to their relationship to the extent that one day he had decided unilaterally to call it off.

"I don't have a choice. My parents object strongly to my establishing a relationship with a divorcee. Let's not see each other from now onwards." He made his stand very firmly.

Petrina reacted very badly to this abrupt and unilateral decision. At a time when she was in dire need of emotional support she could not quite accept his sudden change of mind. She had taken his initial promise of affection very seriously and held it deeply in her heart. In fact she had considered it a vow that was too serious to be broken. This sudden withdrawal of love was neither tenable nor conceivable from her perspective.

In the end, the shock from the bombshell was too much for her. This second emotional trauma was as bad, if not worse than the one Joshua had earlier inflicted on her. She became sad, depressed and felt emotionally torn apart. Coping with a second relationship-related trauma quickly became problematic.

From the moment of the breakup, Petrina's true self went into hiding. She became alienated from her current and past experiences. Unfortunately there was traumatic censoring of her memory of certain aspects of the experience of her relationship with Aaron, such that some parts were forgotten while others were substituted by an idealized version of the truth.

Life was harsh and her choices were limited. She needed to survive the unbearable life experience but found herself incapable of managing it. Feeling hurt and confused, she was rapidly falling apart as tension was building up within her.

The impact of her traumatic forgetting was escalating while emptiness and sadness was rapidly eating into her life. She had no safe people to talk to about her experiences. She started to feel dissociated and numb. This eventually manifested as episodic blackouts. She started experiencing syncope during the lunch hour while at work. Life had become misery and darkness ever since.

The above story was slowly unfolding in Petrina's memory bank as the dialogue between Aaron and her continued in the void deck. At the point when Aaron was explaining the circumstances under which they broke off, she suddenly woke up.

Until now she had been meticulously making notes in her diary to capture the content of their conversation. Suddenly one statement struck her deeply. If anything, it snapped her right out of her amnesic state!

"It is not your fault. Nor is it my fault, and the breakup is not a big deal anyway," Aaron said in a light-hearted manner.

Petrina resented very badly the way Aaron presented his justification. After all, he was the one who had wanted the relationship in the first place. Although he was supposedly under parental pressure, he could have at least offered to meet up with her less often until her divorce proceedings were completed. She didn't see the haste to break off abruptly and completely. She did not even have the chance to meet his parents.

With the light-hearted statement from Aaron, Petrina suddenly woke up and understood the source of her dissociative amnesia. It was the disappointment of having placed her complete trust in someone whom she thought was rescuing her from the depths of despair. She had hoped that he was the ultimate person whom she could depend upon as a life partner. It was also the horror of a repeat experience of another romantic partner giving her "empty promises" and ending in another failed relationship.

In this moment of fury she ripped the page on which she had been writing off from her diary. She next tore it repeatedly into multiple pieces and flung the paper pieces at Aaron's face.

Next, dizziness came on. There was a ringing sound in her ears and she began to feel faint. This was followed quickly by a blackout. As she sank to her feet, she knocked and bruised her shins. She recalled recovering quickly from her blackout, but only to faint and fall again afterwards. What was disappointing and frustrating was the fact that Aaron had allowed her to fall each time without lifting a finger to catch her. It was unimaginable to her that a man whom she had always cherished as a lover and regarded as a perfect gentleman in her mind could be doing this to her at such a vulnerable moment!

*****

I was sitting in my hospital office that morning, busy with the writing of my medical reports. It was 10:40 am. My mobile phone rang and Aaron's number appeared on the display. I was surprised as I was unaware of what had gone on that morning at his house.

"Hello," I answered curiously.

"Dr. Mack, I am Aaron." It was a flustered voice. "Sorry I had to call you so suddenly, but I thought maybe you can help."

"What's the matter?" I was getting intrigued.

"It's Petrina." He sounded stressed. "She is at my place right now."

My heart sank. I had not expected Petrina to be that daring.

"She came to look for me this morning at my house," Aaron continued. "I have been talking to her and helping her to recall her memory, but now she has broken down and is crying away. I am afraid I cannot handle her."

Over the phone, I could hear someone crying agitatedly and in emotional turmoil. The voice was recognizable as belonging to Petrina.

"Did she come alone?" I asked worriedly.

"Yes, unfortunately, and there's no one to help me."

"Hmm ..." I hesitated. "Can I speak to her then?"

There was a pause with some muffled voices in the background, and then Aaron's voice returned. "I am afraid she is too emotional to talk at this stage."

I was thinking fast.

"Well ... maybe you can call her mother to fetch her home. She is probably at work now, but you can try her mobile hand phone." After the incident when Petrina was caught helplessly alone in Hougang Avenue 3, and stuck with a loss of memory of her own home address, I had taken down her mother's mobile phone number as a precaution. I fumbled through my phone database, retrieved the number and gave it verbally to Aaron.

I sat back on my office chair and gave a sigh. I was mulling over the incident and trying to figure out what might possibly happen next.

Twenty minutes later, Aaron called back. He sounded even more distressed.

"Dr. Mack, her mum hasn't answered my call. Petrina is still with me here and I don't know what to do with her ... Oh, wait a minute, I think she wants to speak to you."

There was a sense of relief in the tone of his voice as he handed the phone to Petrina.

"Dr. Mack, I have remembered everything now," Petrina said in a tremulous voice and in a very emotional manner. She then burst out crying as she handed the phone back to Aaron.

"Okay, Aaron, she does sound very emotional." Keeping my cool, I said: "Why don't you give her a bit of time to settle down and after that bring her to see me in hospital. She has a clinic appointment with me today anyway."

"Errh … how do I go about doing it?"

"It is not safe for her to come alone, because she can blackout anytime. Do you mind accompanying her to my clinic?"

"Well …" There was a moment of silence at the other end. I sensed some hesitancy. "Errr … okay, but to which part of the hospital should I send her?"

Before I could answer, Aaron continued meekly. "I have another appointment to attend to after this." It was clear that he was trying to distance himself from Petrina's dilemma.

"Oh, I see …" I felt disappointed. "In that case can you just accompany her to the taxi drop-off point at the entrance to Block 3 of the hospital. I will take care of her from there."

I sighed. What I couldn't understand was how Petrina could get emotionally entangled with someone who did not seem to show any reasonable level of caring or love for her. I gave another sigh as I returned my hand phone back to my pouch. In her current physical state, I thought I had better meet her at the drop-off point of the hospital entrance. At least I could catch a glimpse of what the man called Aaron looked like.

I estimated that they would take approximately 15 to 20 minutes to arrive by taxi. At around 11:15 am I left my office and start walking towards the lift at the seventh floor.

Once inside the lift, Aaron called to say that he had already arrived in the outpatient department at Clinic C. As the lift reached level one, I hurried out and walked briskly towards the clinic. As I reached the basement level via the elevator, someone called my name. I turned around and saw a tall, tanned-looking man. He was about 5 feet 9 inches in height, wearing a reddish-brown T-shirt, gray-colored shorts and sandals. He was walking towards me and his face looked glum.

"Hi, I am Aaron." He introduced himself.

So I finally met the man who was at the core of Petrina's woes. He was the contributor to all her nightmarish attacks and misery. He was also the trigger for her to snap out of trance each time during therapy. Comparatively, his contribution to Petrina's trauma appeared to have had a greater impact than what came from her husband, Joshua.

He spoke clearly, slowly and in an unruffled manner. This was despite all the stress and drama he had experienced from Petrina for the past hour and a half at his residence. I was impressed by his composure. I also noticed that he was alone. Instinctively I looked around and Petrina was nowhere in sight.

"Petrina has gone to the washroom." He saw my eyes searching and explained. Then he pointed in the direction of the ladies' restroom that was located beside the elevator.

"You came fast," I remarked.

"We came by taxi. It took only ten minutes but she blacked out three times on our way here."

"Aren't you in a hurry to leave?" I asked.

"No." He shook his head.

"How's Petrina now?" I asked.

Without answering me he searched his shirt pocket. "By the way, I thought I should pass these to you, in case you may find them useful."

His left hand grabbed something from his shirt pocket and took out a handful of pieces of torn paper. There were sixteen pieces in all, and I recognized them immediately as having been torn from a page in Petrina's diary. They were from the page she had thrown in Aaron's face earlier. However, he subsequently retrieved the pieces from the floor in case they provide useful clues for me to assist in her memory recovery.

"Thanks," I said as I took the paper pieces from him and quickly tucked them safely out of sight. I had an uneasy feeling that Petrina might appear any moment and her tendency to blackout might be triggered once more by the sight of her diary page in pieces.

"But, what actually happened earlier on at your place?" I asked.

"Well, Petrina came knocking on my door this morning, asking for help to recover her memory. I talked to her at length and … as she was regaining her memory she got very agitated and she fainted."

As Aaron was talking, I saw, at a distance, Petrina coming out from the toilet. Once past the door she felt weak and was trying hard to support herself against the wall. My heart sank. I sensed that another syncope was coming on soon. True enough, she started to slide down the wall and fall. I rushed forward. Just as I was reaching her, she was at the last part of her downslide against the wall and sank to the ground. All this happened within a couple of seconds. Being a public area in a busy hospital, this aroused attention and caused a commotion.

I called for help. The clinic assistants hurried to look for a trolley and the nurses quickly covered her temporarily with a bed sheet while waiting for the trolley to arrive. I stayed by her with my index and middle fingers on her radial pulse throughout. Her breathing was regular and I noticed that she was struggling to lift her eyelids but was too tired to open them wide. This gave me an indication that she should be regaining full consciousness soon.

When the assistants finally came with a trolley, the nurses carried her up and placed her on it. She was then transferred into the privacy of one of the consultation rooms. She needed rest and we left her on the trolley for the moment. What disgusted me was the fact that Aaron had stayed away at a distance all this while when everyone else was trying to help.

From what I had learned from Petrina, Aaron was a very polite and courteous person, and had always behaved as a perfect gentleman in public. During the two months when they were out dating, she had noticed whenever they frequented a fast-food restaurant such as McDonald's, Aaron would voluntarily help to clear the dining tables of food trays left behind by departed customers. He was someone that, if a table was found dirty and even if he did not intend to sit there, he would still volunteer to clear the food trays. He was such a person that if someone had fallen down on the road, he would be the first to go and help.

With the foregoing account, it was inconceivable therefore that Aaron could have actively refrained from helping his own former girlfriend who had fainted and fallen right in front of his eyes. She would never have dreamed that he could stay motionless all this while, leaving her alone on the floor without helping. Clearly he had wanted to dissociate himself from the scene of commotion.

Fifteen minutes later, Petrina was settling down quietly in the room with a clinic nurse next to her. There was a disgusted look on her face while she was struggling to open her eyes and recover from her syncope.

She asked in a bitter tone: "What the hell is Aaron doing outside?"

As she hadn't completely recovered, I avoided replying. Instead I allowed her to calm down and let her know that I would be leaving her with the nurse for a while as I looked for Aaron outside.

Soon I found him standing sheepishly outside at one corner in the public waiting area. He had made no attempt whatsoever to help when he saw Petrina fainting and falling down. When several of us were busy transferring her to the trolley, he had actively stayed away from the scene of action. The sight of his aloofness suddenly reminded me of the symbolism behind Petrina's vivid dream of 7 December. In that dream he was the man who had not bothered to help her when she was desperately trying to get out of a room in which she was locked (Fig. 9).

We resumed our conversation from where we were interrupted. Aaron narrated his version of the story. He had originally met Petrina on 5 July because a mutual friend had asked Petrina to pass a box of chocolates and a thank-you card to him. He saw that as Petrina's excuse to befriend him. He confirmed that they went to see *Karate Kids* in Tampines Mall that evening. After the show they had dinner together in a Japanese restaurant. He claimed that thereafter Petrina fell for him. They started a relationship to which his mother eventually objected. So he decided to call it off to ease the family tension. He did not expect that the decision would have such a devastating impact on her.

As he talked, his nasal sinuses were getting moist and I could hear that he was beginning to sniff. For a moment I believed that his emotions might be building up.

At that stage my assessment of Aaron was that it was unlikely that I could get further help from him beyond what he had already done for Petrina. Nor did he seem eager to wait for Petrina to wake up and bid her goodbye. I made a quick decision and spoke to him frankly.

"Okay, Petrina is recovering from her blackout and she may come round anytime now." I then reminded Aaron, "It may not be a good idea for you to be around when she's awake. I do not want to risk her seeing your presence and getting upset. It's best you leave now." I put it across to him in a sincere tone.

"Thanks, Dr. Mack, for what you've done. We shall keep in touch." There was a sign of uneasiness on his face, but he sounded relieved nonetheless. He briskly disappeared from my sight without hesitation.

I gave a further sigh and returned to the consultation room to follow up on Petrina. She had come round by now. The clinic nurse Faridah had earlier helped her out from the trolley and assisted her onto a chair. She was now alert but visibly depressed. Faridah brought in a cup of warm water for her.

There was a long and uneasy silence in the room. I took my seat at the consultation table while she shifted herself to the patient's chair facing me. She took one sip of the warm water and stared miserably at the floor in front of her. I sat face to face with her and decided it was best to remain silent.

The first two minutes passed ... she said nothing. There were signs of anger and frustration on her face. I actively refrained from talking. Another minute passed, and she still did not speak. The furrows over her eyebrows were gradually loosening up.

After the fourth minute, she gave a sigh. Then she lifted up her head and I saw the bitterness in her facial expression.

"I now remember everything that has happened," she said in a bitter tone. "He's hurt me badly."

"I know," I replied softly.

"Where is he now?" she asked.

"I have sent him off while you were recovering," I responded slowly, watching her expression. "I didn't want you to see him and feel upset again at this point in time. Anyway, he said he has another appointment to attend to."

There was several seconds of silence.

"A bag of lies, that man ... all empty promises," she said angrily. "Don't know why I got involved with him. He is so disappointing!"

"You're upset." I paused. "It has been a difficult time for you ... but at least he didn't physically abuse you like Joshua did."

"But this is worse, isn't it?" she said defiantly, holding up her head sideways to her left, looking at me. I could feel the hurt radiating from her piercing glance.

My heart ached. I stayed in eye contact with her but decided to say nothing. At a time like this I believed silence would be more helpful.

"Imagine that all this while I have been unwell because of him. I should not have trusted him," she said regretfully.

We retreated back into silence once more. The minutes ticked by. The energy level in the room was high. Deep down, I was wondering where the awkward situation was leading us to.

Chapter Twelve

The Breakthrough

Forgiveness is the key that unlocks the door of resentment and the handcuffs of hate. It is a power that breaks the chains of bitterness and the shackles of selfishness.

– William Arthur Ward

It seemed like a long time that Petrina and I were facing each other. In the midst of the commotion and drama when she had fainted in front of the toilet, I intuitively sensed that Eileen, my psychic friend, had remembered me. She told me earlier that she had been suffering from an upper respiratory tract infection recently. While consulting her family doctor that morning, she had sent me a wonderful SMS message.

"Good morning, I am at the doctor's clinic. I have called my prayer group to pray for your patient and for all the angels to pray and assist you today."

The message brightened up my mood. It came at a time when Petrina was struggling to overcome her anger and when I was thinking of ways to help her.

I was still sitting in the consultation room quietly praying for Petrina's recovery. While silently saying my prayers, I suddenly got an unmistakable feeling that she was turning around.

Petrina's body tension was easing. Her breathing had become more regular and the furrows on her forehead had faded. She looked more comfortable now and her bitter complexion was disappearing. Her friendly look returned and she seemed to be letting go of things. A rapid transformational process was taking place. Her facial expression was lightening up and the positive energy level in the room was on the rise.

Half an hour later, Petrina resumed her composure. She decidedly said: "It is really pointless to get upset over the man. It's all over."

"I understand you." I affirmed her decision and felt a little relieved.

"I think I want to go home now," she surprised me by saying suddenly.

"All by yourself?" I hesitated.

"Yes," she asserted firmly.

For a moment my eyes were focused on her facial expression and I did not know what to say.

"I will take a cab home myself. It should be okay." She seemed to read my mind.

After staring at her hesitantly for a while I told myself to trust my own instincts. "Alright. I will let you go back on your own on one condition."

"Yes?" She was wondering what I wanted.

"You promise to call me once you reach home safely?"

She looked at me with a forced smile and nodded her head.

I walked her to the taxi stand once more. Silence prevailed.

"Take care," I said softly. A taxi decelerated and was braking at the waiting lot in front of us. She turned around and gave a touching smile. It was a smile that reaffirmed my feelings of confidence that she was already on her way to recovery.

It was noon as I stared at the taxi driving off. I meditated over her sudden change in mood. It was intuitive to me that healing had commenced and taken place. I had a strong premonition that this moment had marked a turning point of her illness.

At around 1:00 pm I received a SMS message from Petrina to say that she had reached home safely. It was a wonderful feeling.

For the first time in three weeks, I felt really relaxed. I returned to my office and anticipated more good news soon.

On reaching home, Petrina sat down and quietly reflected over the morning experience. There was a Buddhist altar at her home. As she took a seat in front of the altar, she played the meditation CD that I had given her earlier. The soothing music sounded in her ears but she was now able to listen to it with her heart rather than with her mind.

She had been feeling a lot of psychological pain and imbalance when the inner elements within her were unconnected. However, now her mental chatter was dispelling and she was slowly finding her way to the spiritual dimension. The fragments of her inner self were slowly merging together in successively greater wholes.

It was a mood of peaceful quiet. While she was meditating, she asked herself several questions: Why am I so miserable? Why ask myself so many questions? It is all over now and why not be forgiving to myself? And if I can forgive myself and forgive Aaron, then my life will be much better off. Why is it that I have to compare myself and other people? Shouldn't I be content with what I have now because that would make things a lot easier?

The search for answers to her own questions was a tremendous help. The silence within her was like the steady flame of a candle in still air. She suddenly experienced a release of energy and a sense of wellbeing. It was a feeling as if her dark night had transformed into a morning of brightness. The process of meditation had allowed her to gain dignified self-possession and made forgiveness possible.

It did not take too long for conflict to vanish and mental scattering to give way to unity. Petrina's acceptance of her situation had allowed her to acknowledge the anger and resentment that had hitherto been preventing forgiveness. For the first time she sensed a more profound depth of meaning in her life.

Her flow of thoughts continued placidly. The turning of her attention inward made her thoughts more active and insistent. Subsequently Petrina recalled what was developing in her mind at that fateful moment. "Maybe indirectly the God I was offering at home is sending me a message that it's time for me to move on and do not bother about unnecessary stuff."

It was a state of intense but relaxed alertness developing within her. Insights seemed to be flowing into the space she had created. She had finally developed an understanding of the feelings of the hurt and heartache surrounding the need for forgiveness.

At one stage she started to quote examples. "I saw a lot of documentaries on television. I happened to see this lady from Africa. She is suffering from illness and yet she is struggling to live another day until she would see her children grow up. So I ask myself, if she has the kind of ability to do that why is it that I am so healthy and yet cannot do it? There must be a reason why God made me that way."

The afternoon marked a turning point in her life. Her memories were returning promptly. She remembered the high hopes she had pinned on Aaron to help her turn a new leaf in her life while she was undergoing divorce. She had recalled how her disappointment with him had earlier wrecked her emotions and sent her on a journey of misery. She remembered the identities of all her friends and colleagues who had been objects of her amnesia. She also remembered where and how she had misplaced her medical leave certificate and the circumstances leading to her overlooking the submission of that important document. She could also remember, in detail, all the atrocious behavior from her supervisor Shirlene whom she had been putting up with. Furthermore she could recall all the people and events that had triggered her blackouts in the recent months. But everything was over now.

She had come to accept who she was and no longer judge herself as harshly for her shortcomings like before. Most important of all, by learning to forgive, she had taken a major step towards her acceptance of the spiritual realm.

Love was what she lived by, and yet it was also what she had earlier blinded and tortured herself by.

The ability to examine the meaning of love from the standpoint of human essence was a joy. She had understood that love was objective and not distorted by individual bias. Hence she was able to identify with other people without being overwhelmed. She could now see how love was impregnated with intelligent comprehension and how she could free others who were touched by it.

About two hours later, the bleeper of my hand phone sounded. It was 2:48 pm and it was a landmark message from Petrina:

"Thanks for everything you've done for me, Dr. Mack ... It's a journey of life in which I've finally understood what is meant by 'Let Go'. Rather than hating and carrying guilt, I've learned to be forgiving ... If Aaron were to contact you please let him know I'm thankful that he helped me to recover ... I don't hate or blame him if he's willing to keep in contact as friends. My door is always open for him ... Hating a person takes up too much energy and it's not worth it ... Since God didn't take me away there must be a reason. So I am grateful that I met Aaron. He brought me lots of misery but indirectly made me stronger than before."

This was perhaps the most beautiful and encouraging message that I have ever received from Petrina since the day I encountered her as a patient. Love had evoked her courage to step forward and her confidence to plunge into the new. It had helped her to melt her blocks and to untie her knots. She had finally brought everything to a closure after two weeks of intensive hypnosis and regression therapy.

Petrina had rediscovered herself. A mysterious inner barrier had just loosened. In that moment the most exquisite realization entered her awareness. I resonated with her statement that hating people was unproductive. I remembered that someone once compared hating people to the act of burning down your own house to get rid of a rat. It was a joy to communicate with her over the phone. I emphasized the need for her to move on in life because happiness would only be held back if she continued to be tied down to her past.

That evening Petrina reflected and wrote in her journal:

Tuesday, 14 December
⇨ *7:40 pm*

Went to Aaron's office to confront him ... He told me lots of lies till today. I understand why he is not willing to meet Dr. Mack. Just a liar like Joshua. Think back to commit suicide for him and lost Fabian my best friend was not worth it ... It doesn't matter ...Without him I wouldn't recover so soon. Though he has hurt me but without him I would not be stronger then before. Can't totally blame him. If I did not give him the chance to start the relationship it will not end up like that. It's a life learning stage so I've chosen to forgive him and keep him as friend ... hating a person is too tiring, not worth it. Aaron can only look back and regret that he didn't cherish me. Though my love for him is still very strong but I believe one day I will be able to get over him. Time will heal the wounds.

In the meanwhile Aaron had sheepishly asked me to keep him updated on Petrina's clinical progress. He seemed to be feeling bad about having left her all alone in the hospital and going home by himself. I informed him that she was doing well and already on her road to recovery. I also reassured him that from my clinical evaluation of her rate of recovery, she was most unlikely to bother him any further.

He felt relieved and wrote me a long message.

"I really do hope those memories she recovered do more good than harm for her. It's depressing to see her in this state, but like you said, she should get better day by day. Thank you for reaching out to her. Let's hope life will continue to get better for her. You have been wonderful, Dr. Mack. I'm glad that she came looking for me today and having to meet you personally. She did send me two messages afterwards, letting me know that she remembered everything, but I didn't reply as I don't wish to further complicate things. Have a Blessed Christmas."

As I read and pondered over Aaron's message I wondered if the relationship between the two was really over as they had claimed. There was a nudging feeling that something unexpected was yet to happen again soon. However, I couldn't get a handle on it.

On reaching home that evening after work I felt physically tired, but emotionally in high spirits. I had not experienced such a feeling of tiredness for a very long time. As I sank into the comfort and softness of my sofa, I logged on to the Internet and proceeded to update Nurse Beatrice, Sister Louise and Eileen about what had happened today. As usual Beatrice was upbeat about all successes in hypnotherapy.

"Very dramatic and tiring," she commented, "but it's worth the time and effort if it makes someone's life better ... Petrina is very right; being angry takes up a lot of energy. I am happy for you that she's getting better now."

Beatrice added a very encouraging remark to her message. "Being an effective hypnotist is kind of like being an effective hunter ... Mastery is having the right technique for the client that you are assisting."

The last sentence of her message actually pertained to a short, insightful story that her fellow hypnotherapist friends from

IMDHA (International Medical and Dental Hypnotherapy Association) had shared with her. She emailed the story to me. I loved reading it a lot and called it the "Parable of the Hunter". It was both apt and inspiring.

Parable of the Hunter

Once, there was a tribe ... and in this tribe was the son of the best hunter in the village. He adored his father and wanted to be just like him. So each day, he took his bow and arrow out and practiced and practiced and practiced. So accurate was his aim that none of the other boys in the village would even try to compete with him because he would always shoot straight and true and would win every shooting competition.

Finally, his father agreed to take him on a hunt. He was overjoyed. He got up early in the morning and took his bow and grabbed an arrow and went to meet his father. When he saw his father, he was shocked. On his back were 3 or 4 different bows and at least 100 arrows. The boy was confused. "Father ... Why do you bring so many arrows ... you are the best hunter in the village. I have brought only ONE arrow and ONE bow. Surely you are a better shot than I am. Why do you have so many arrows and bows?"

The Father replied ... "I am the best hunter in the village because I have so many different arrows. When it is raining ... I use this arrow ... when the air is dry I have a special arrow for that also. This arrow is for shooting birds out of the sky, and this one is for shooting fish in the river. I have a bow for long range, and a bow for close up. I have one for rabbits, one for deer and one for bear. Because I always have the exact bow and the exact arrow for the exact game I am hunting for, I am always successful. And that is why I am the best hunter in the village."

Sister Louise was extremely happy at the news of Petrina's recovery. In many ways she was proud that she had taken the initiative to intervene in the management of her patient's illness and provided the necessary support to make therapy possible.

Eileen, on her part, also came back with equally encouraging words:

"Praise God and all His angels for their help. You will be able to help her to be a stronger person with confidence to face the new world. But she still needs you so please look after her for a little more. Hugs, you did a great job."

Those words "she still needs you" caught my attention. I had always taken Eileen's words and advice seriously. Reading between the lines of Eileen's message, I sensed that Petrina's "hero's journey" might not have ended just yet.

*****

Back at home in the evening, Petrina was sleeping very soundly and peacefully. It was the first time in three years that she had fallen asleep easily and enjoyed uninterrupted, quality sleep. She felt like a bird that had pecked her way out of an egg.

The following morning she felt rested, and it was a feeling that she had not experienced for a long time. It was the day when the world appeared different. With relief, she saw that all the distress and emptiness that had previously been so painful had disappeared overnight.

There was a bright golden haze on the horizon as she looked out of her bedroom window. The air seemed to be alive. She had a wonderful feeling that it was going to be a beautiful day. She felt strong and confident that all her psychological problems had been dealt with. Everything seemed to be going her way.

After breakfast she went back to bed and spent much of the rest of the day sleeping without pharmacological aid. Physically she continued to experience tiredness. It was as if she had a lot of catching up to do with her sleep, but this did not worry her.

Tuesday, 14 December

⇨ *10:07 pm*

It's been a very long time since I had a good sleep. It's wonderful sleeping without any medicine ... but waking up in pain physically because I've fainted a few times. Guess when I fell Aaron didn't catch hold of me ... Disappointed though ... he used to be very sweet and protective but after what happened yesterday, he's just so not worth it. Especially when I see the smile on his face when I'm in that condition. Well, just proved that he's a hypocrite ...

Looking back at what happened yesterday, part of me hopes that he'll at least be gentlemanly enough to stay until he sees that I'm alright and send me back home ... It seems like he doesn't feel a bit remorseful of what he has done. Anyway I believe one day when he looks back he'll definitely regret. It's not easy to find someone who genuinely loves him. In my case I've given love to both Joshua and Aaron; it's just that they don't cherish what they have. The moment I recall everything yesterday and realize Aaron has been telling lies which have no intention of helping me to recover, my love for him slowly dies off ...

I'm confident I'll get over him very soon. I've always told myself to cherish what I have before it's too late. As for Aaron, guess when he looks back and wants to make up for what he did I'm no longer there. It's like a cycle. What goes round comes round. I've chosen to be forgiving.

Petrina felt like a different person. As someone who had got herself unstuck from the problems of life, she felt both light at heart as well as happy in outlook. While she had not forgotten her hurt-laden memories, she could now calmly recall them and was able to reframe those past experiences very differently. The last three months of her life had been awful, but experiencing the pain in the manner she went through had been most liberating and crucial to her healing process. She had replaced resentment and bitterness with positive thoughts and feelings. While part of the inner hurt remained, enmity was now substituted with amity. Her clarity of mind had shown her the way to her source of inner peace and inspiration.

She had figured out a fundamental principle. The human mind was like a butterfly that assumed the color of the foliage it settled on. Likewise her thoughts acted on her in profound ways and had newly defined her universe. With this she was amazed at the speed of her recovery.

"I am still quite puzzled with how I managed to recover so fast. It is like an overnight thing," she recalled.

Ever since she sent out to me the message of forgiveness that day, she no longer experienced any more blackouts. She was also completely free from depression. Her family members were as astonished as she was. The news of her dramatic recovery had quickly gone round her social circle and attracted a stream of friends and visitors to her house.

*****

It was the afternoon of Thursday, 16 December, and was Petrina's 18th day of therapy. She turned up at my clinic at 3:30 pm but this time with a cheerful and shining complexion.

She was wearing a black, knee-length skirt. The dress appeared glossy and attractive, with spaghetti straps over both shoulders. She was smiling and was beaming with happiness and a goddess-like charm. She wore a thin necklace with a small pendant around her neck. She had teased her long hair carefully and applied make-up to create a hint of a blush that made her look youthful and enchanting. She had swept her mascara until her eyelashes were rich and her eyes sultry. It was a marked contrast to the frail countenance and mask-like appearance when I first met her. Shining in beauty and sparkling with confidence, she stepped into my clinic.

We had a most enjoyable and fruitful conversation. We talked on many related topics including the lessons in healing that we had jointly experienced together. Her insomnia had vanished overnight and she had been sleeping both peacefully and soundly. In fact she had slept continuously for 13 hours at a stretch the night before, and felt very much improved in her mental state after waking up.

She admitted that she had never truly felt happy in her life until now. She could comfortably recall all the unpleasant memories she had previously repressed. She could recollect all her emotional traumas and share her painful experiences without hesitation and fear. After sharing them she would just dismiss those memories with a shrug and smile. She assured me of her confidence in resuming work in the ophthalmology clinic upon expiry of her medical leave. Furthermore, handling her supervisor Shirlene had ceased to be an issue.

She next recollected her childhood days, her rebellious behavior and how she survived within a dysfunctional family. She described her earlier feelings of her lack of security as a result of which she thought that by marrying early she would be able to depend on a man to give her the needed security.

She clarified my doubt about the circumstances surrounding her third pregnancy. It happened at the time when she had already initiated divorce proceedings and moved out of the house. One day she came back to pick up a forgotten item and bumped into Joshua. In a moment of desire he had forced intercourse on her.

We then talked about Aaron again. She felt safe enough to openly share her sentiments and inner feelings. As a person, Petrina had understood him as someone who "preferred to have more family life". After their relationship breakup, he decided that he would spend more time with his own family. Rather than just working as an employee for a management consulting company, he left to set up his own business. While he was still doing market research and planning, his sister needed help and he went over to his sister's company. Not long after that, his sister's company ran into serious financial difficulties. Thereafter he started his own cleaning business which his father agreed to fund.

Thursday, 16th December
⇨ *11:15 pm*

Today I went for Dr. Mack's appointment, feeling relaxed and happy. Finally all the nightmares are over ☺.

I've always heard from people saying being Happy or Not is your choice, and never really understood what it meant. Now after so much trauma and lessons learned, I really understood the meaning of it. Most of the time many people tend to take things for granted, asking for more, always complaining, comparing why other people are having this and that ... why is it that I can't have? Which makes their lives difficult for themselves. I used to be like them but now I've changed. The new me feels that human beings must learn to be contented for what they have. Don't expect too much, so even when you don't meet your expectation, you won't feel really upset. The funny thing is that most people don't see or cherish what they have in front of them, but when they look back they start to regret ... So why make life so difficult for yourself?

I believe in karma and reincarnation. If human life span is averaging around 65 years then how many rounds we need to go through the process to be a human again? If that's the case why not choose to live life to the fullest, be a happy person? You'll never know what will happen tomorrow.

I noticed Petrina was particularly open about herself, her past and the changes she had been through. I therefore took the opportunity to explore the more personal aspects of her life.

"By the way, does Joshua have any Thai friends?" I avoided divulging the content of my earlier conversation with Eileen at this stage.

"Yes, a lot in fact," she readily responded. Over the next few minutes a long story emerged.

"He used to hang out with many of his Thai friends because he has business dealings with them, but I was never introduced to any of them. After we got married we used to live in an eerie shop/house apartment inside which he had an altar on which he placed the statue of a Thai god. He prayed regularly and a lot of funny things seemed to happen in the house after that. For instance, his prayers seemed to attract a lot of centipedes. I don't know why. These are not small centipedes but big ones, about five to six inches long each ... very scary. A year back he started putting a Thai statue inside the car that he drove, and I remember that was the time our relationship started to deteriorate."

The information was startling. It was amazingly consistent with what Eileen had communicated to me earlier. I continued to probe.

"Were there any other funny things associated with Joshua's worship?"

"Yes ... very frightening things. Three years ago one evening, around 9:55 pm I saw an entity lying on our bed dressed in black and appeared like a Vietnamese woman, with long black fingernails. I can't remember how long she was around, but she never came back. Ever since that time, my insomnia started."

It was a very intriguing dialogue. I had been asking myself: Had Petrina really been struggling against a charm all this while?

Chapter Thirteen

Unfinished Business

*In traumatic deaths especially – sudden or horrible deaths – we
have no way to come to terms with our lives or our death ... If we
die incomplete, we leave that lifetime with what Dr. Woolger calls
"unfinished business of the soul". We pass through death's door
carrying our unresolved issues with us and an urge to finish what
we have left undone. These issues begging to be resolved are
what manifest as problems in another lifetime. Unfinished
business propels the memories.*

– Carol Bowman

We ended the session at 5:45 pm. For the first time in the past three weeks, she was going home by bus instead of by taxi. As I was sending her off, it suddenly occurred to me to ask something which I previously never had a chance to ask while she was ill.

"By the way, Petrina, have you realized all along that I am not a psychiatrist?"

She smiled broadly. "Yeah, my brother asked me about it the other day. He was wondering why on earth is a general surgeon performing hypnotherapy on his sister!"

I smiled back and stood quietly at the hospital entrance as I watched her leaving and walking towards the direction of the bus stop. This was one of the most jubilant moments of my life.

As she slowly faded into the distance I reflected over the last three weeks of my therapy experience with her. She was someone whose life I had made a difference to with regression therapy. It was an inner dialogue with herself that I had got her to engage in. Through that she was availed of the truth that had been hidden and forgotten within herself. From the brim of despair and suicide, I had brought her back to her stable, confident and hopeful self. She had chosen to revive her courage and determination to move on to a meaningful life. She had learned how to rely on herself rather than being influenced by others. She seemed to have found a solution to her problem at a level higher than the one where the problem was residing.

It was a level of satisfaction that I had never experienced in the past three decades of my surgical career. With all the disease pathologies that I had successfully treated with surgery or medication, the sense of pride and achievement had never been as profound.

Her nightmares were all behind her. She continued to update me closely on the progress of her health status and her day-to-day emotions.

Fig.16 : "All nightmares are over now."

She felt cheerful, tranquil and had become truly happy in her life. She had released the resentment, hatred and bitterness of unforgiveness and had replaced them with love. Insomnia had ceased to be an issue. She enjoyed deep and restful sleep and was rapidly catching up with what she had missed in the last three years of life. However, with her enjoyable long sleeping hours she was beginning to suffer from an aching neck pain!

Petrina was now committed to advance a better world. Over the next four days while she was rapidly recuperating, she kept herself busy at home by packing her belongings. Now she began to realize that she had a lot of things in her possession that she no longer needed. These included new dresses which she had previously bought but never wore and didn't intend to. She had no idea what to do with them and was wondering if she should discard them.

On 18 December, while packing her clothes, she found a Mickey and Minnie Mouse jigsaw puzzle in her closet. It was a Christmas gift that she had bought in August, for Aaron. She had kept it in her wardrobe and totally forgotten about it ever since she fell ill. She deliberated over what she should do with the gift now. Should she discard, or not discard?

After much thought, she decided to send the gift to Aaron anyway. Since the original intention was to make the present specially for him, she felt that the gift rightfully belonged to him and no one else. What had happened to their relationship in the interim was a separate issue and should not impact on the genuineness of her original intention. She was psychologically prepared that even if Aaron should ultimately choose to throw the gift away that would be his choice and would not bother her. At least, by passing the gift to him, she would have the chance of delivering the message she wanted to pass to him at the time the present was prepared. After all, if the gift was meant for him, it would be meaningless to give it to anyone else.

She wrote an explanatory letter to tell Aaron the reason for her decision to send the gift to him at this stage. At the same time she thanked him for having helped her to recover her memory, and apologized for the inconvenience as well as the anxiety she had caused him. Next, she asked her good friend Bernard for a favor – to help to deliver the gift to Aaron's residence!

"Why?" Bernard asked with astonishment.

"To finish what I started," she said in a determined tone. After all, she believed that forgiveness meant that she did not have to carry the emotional baggage of her experience with him. Being unfinished business, it was her duty to see it to completion.

The idea of forgiving a person was, in Petrina's perspective, equivalent to letting go of her Self so as to move on to a better future. She really wanted to get over the whole incident and let Aaron know that she had succeeded in doing so without blaming him. She felt it was particularly important for her to thank him for helping her in her recovery process, despite the reluctance he exhibited. She did not want to hold him responsible for the experience she had been through and preferred to bring the whole matter to a closure. She knew very well that it was inappropriate for her to be seen physically with Aaron again because that would potentially inflict trauma on his family members. Hence, she approached her good friend Bernard for help.

"Nobody would ever do such a thing!" Bernard said in exasperation. "He did all those rubbish things to you and in the end you still send him a present! If I were you I would either burn the whole present or perhaps even burn some joss papers for him instead!" Burning joss papers is common in traditional Chinese religious practices and is practiced to venerate the dead. However, the phrase is also commonly used as a figure of speech to express disgust for someone who is disliked.

Despite his verbal protests, Bernard eventually agreed to deliver the present on Petrina's behalf. Aaron was not at home at the time of the delivery but the present eventually reached him via his next-door neighbour. To Petrina's satisfaction, he gracefully acknowledged receipt of the gift and returned her a thank-you message.

By now Petrina had not only worked through her pain but had also managed to sort out and reconcile her outstanding conflicts. Her personality had awakened to the potential of her soul. She now decided to turn to the Higher Power to release her remaining patterns of negativity and learn through her wisdom.

On 19 December, Petrina accompanied her parents to pray in ten different Chinese temples in the city. It was a very tiring day in the temples but she felt good about it. This was because she had spent her precious moments with her family. It was a wonderful experience as she allowed spirituality to help her remove her residual pain and extricate her from the claws of depression. In letting go of her pain, she could now choose to embrace unconditional love.

After a busy day, it suddenly dawned on her as to what she should do with her unwanted clothing at home. She decided to send them to the needy. The very idea of making a donation made her upbeat. She felt she could now help other people in addition to helping herself. She had eventually come to understand that love heals everything, and love is an active state. With love she could bring harmony and an active interest in the wellbeing of others. It was an inner ideal form that was trying to manifest itself within her and it came about as she was reconceiving the notions of therapy and personal growth. The release of pent-up emotions and the treatment of her blackouts were no longer an end in itself but a series of steps in a larger process of becoming aware of her emerging life purpose and eliminating obstacles to it.

The next day, she sent her unwanted but new stuff to the charity gift collection center of the community center near her home. It was a wonderful feeling that she experienced (Fig. 17). After four days of packing her room was finally cleared. Emotionally that was the start of her new journey in life.

Fig. 17: "The feeling is wonderful!"

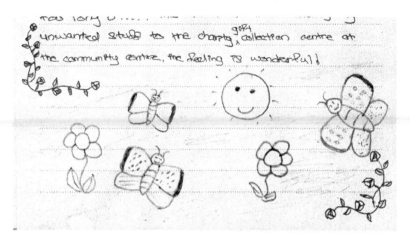

unwanted stuff to the charity collection centre at the community centre, the feeling is wonderful!

Petrina had continued with her journal keeping and I felt that was a wonderful habit that she had developed. By so doing, it would set aside time dedicated for reflection, self-expression and release. By writing freely about the issue that concerned her, she had found herself expressing things not previously thought of.

She was able to express explicitly that which she felt implicitly, thereby clarifying to herself what might have been a confused morass. Journal keeping had always been her emotional anchor since childhood, and each time she made entries she would be reminded of her range of feelings and her old patterns of behavior that she wanted to discard.

It was at this time that she started to share her experience of her past life regression with her second brother. She narrated the past life story that she had visualized under trance to her brother. Although the story showed no obvious link to her current life problem, she nonetheless analyzed the story in detail and sought her brother's perspective with regards to the possible life lessons that might be learned from it.

She was aware that although she had gone through a lot of challenges in this life and still had more to learn. With the past life story in perspective, her brother thought that the guilt part of her seemed to follow a pattern. Her failure to overcome her guilt feelings leading to her suicide attempt in the present life was in many ways a parallel with what had happened in her past life. In her past life it was also her guilt resulting of the murder of the past life Empress that she had difficulty overcoming. Likewise she also ended up in suicide in that past life. It was an enlightening dialogue.

"It is the same thing that has been repeating again and again and you don't listen," her brother commented. "You have never opened up your ears. It is like you are a very stubborn person. It is like your inner guilt. You know what you have done is partly right and partly wrong, but you can't overcome your guilt."

Petrina was well aware that Fabian was an adult, and that it was his choice to make a decision which he believed was in part an act of dutiful responsibility and in part heroism. Yet the guilt she suffered from losing her good friend while escaping death herself had turned out to be an incapacitating hurdle. She needed to overcome this emotional barrier before moving on.

In the height of their discussion, it suddenly dawned on her that the look and appearance of the past life Emperor was very familiar! It was a moment of truth. She suddenly realized that the Emperor was someone she actually knew and was close to her in her current life!

Petrina still felt a lot of remorse over Fabian, who had died during their jointly planned suicide attempt. That was the time when she felt she had lost all hope in life after one failed marriage followed shortly by a subsequent failed relationship. In the impulse of the moment when Fabian was depressed over the departure of his gay partner, she suggested the coordinated suicide plan. Now that she had survived and Fabian hadn't, it was hard for her to overcome her guilt of contributing to Fabian's death.

Petrina decided to communicate her important revelation to me at the next opportunity. The next day Petrina called me to say that she was keen to meet up to provide an update on her clinical progress. I welcomed her initiative. She arrived at the clinic appearing relaxed and serene. We engaged in a most fascinating dialogue.

Fig. 18: "I have to move on in life."

We reviewed chronologically the whole sequence of events in her illness in detail, ending with her relationship encounter with Aaron. Then she narrated how she had convinced herself to come to terms with her own predicament, to let go and to move on in life. Then she shared with me how happy she had become since her breakthrough a week ago.

"It is only recently that I realize that I have really never been happy before ... never, in my twenty-five years of life. I am as happy as I possibly could be now. Too many things have happened already. So I still think that my choice to face things is very important. If I face it, make my mistake and move on, then my life is much easier ... rather than being unable to handle the situation ... which is what caused the entire trauma and all the guilt."

Next, she recapitulated her emotional trauma that surrounded that part of the relationship with Aaron that she couldn't come to terms with. She recalled how each time, at the very mention of Aaron, either consciously or in her trance state during therapy, her guilt feelings would surface. Each time this happened, the guilt blocked all her memories, triggered her blackouts and snapped her out of hypnosis. She ascertained that it was Aaron's empty promises that had upset her tremendously. This had contributed to her depression even more than what Joshua did.

"I got myself into a repeat situation whereby Joshua had been giving me a lot of empty promises and then Aaron did the same thing again. Remember that once I told you that Aaron said to me that I am the last person he will ever hurt!"

"Which means that you placed high hopes on him at that point in time?"

"Yah ... and then plus Fabian's suicide ... Everything was lumped in together. I was not quite stable at that time and made a mistake which led to Fabian's death. When I look back, Aaron is a man who is not worth the relationship. So, because of such kind of man I did such a stupid thing and Fabian then died and I survived ..." she gave a laugh and discontinued her sentence.

"That is very amazing. I was thinking through your story sequence. Yes, this is a case of emotional and physical trauma alright, but the part that you were really hanging on and couldn't resolve was the part concerning Aaron. On that day when I saw how upset you were with him when you two came to the clinic, I realized that your relationship with him was probably much deeper than I thought."

"Oh ... remember that you took me through my past life regression? Now I want to let you know that the so-called Emperor I saw in my past life was in fact Aaron!" She laughed as she disclosed her latest discovery.

"Really!" I exclaimed in amazement, hardly believing my ears. I held my breath for a moment, and wondered if she was serious.

"When did you find out?"

"It was a few days ago when I was having a talk with my brother about my past life! During the conversation, I suddenly realized who that past life Emperor was and why he had a hold on me!"

That was a terribly exciting revelation. A surge of adrenaline went through my entire body once more. I was not convinced until now that Petrina's problem had in fact originated in a past life. Her revelation had suddenly ignited my interest in her past life. We discussed and postulated how the karmic link between Aaron and her had carried their unfinished business from one life to another. In the end we concluded that it was worthwhile to explore her past life in greater depth at another sitting.

Our interactive session ended at about 5:45 pm, by which time Petrina had to leave because she had a prior arrangement to meet her mum for dinner after work. As I watched her walking away in the direction of the MRT train station, I suddenly got a strong feeling that she had a complex karmic tie with Aaron and that it was a knot that she needed to seriously undo, sooner or later.

The next day, Petrina was alone at home, listening again to the meditation CD that I gave her earlier. A strange emotion came on. Somehow, she had no idea why, she felt like she was being "tied down" by a strange feeling for which she had no explanation. She felt as if some unconscious forces were at work binding her down, and the forces involved Aaron. Later she wrote:

> **Wednesday, 22 December**
> ⇨ *10:13 pm*
> *Although I have forgotten Aaron and moved on but Ummm ... I can say forgive, doesn't mean forget ... My disappointment is still there. Probably it is because a part of me still feels that there's love for Aaron. If you ask me: Why? After what he has done to me! ... I can't explain ... But I believe if I can get over Joshua I can get over him as well, it's just the matter of time. Maybe I have put too high hopes on Aaron, that's why until today the feeling is still there ...*

In the early hours of the next morning, Petrina was awakened by a very weird and disturbing dream! The same Emperor in her past life appeared, and he said to her: "You've promised that we will live and grow old together in the next life, but you've broken the promise. Since you left me without my permission, you shall pay back your next life."

She woke up from the dream in a cold sweat. It was such a vivid dream. Unmistakably she recognized the past-life Emperor as Aaron. Her heart was beating away strongly. How was she going to pay back?

It was a scary dream because it seemed that her karmic issue with Aaron had remained unresolved. Being a past life dream, it probably carried an embedded explanation that accounted for the tenacity of her relationship with Aaron and the reason for her being enmeshed with the strange "tied down" feeling. Although she felt she had already found inner peace and new freedom in her life she was curious as to how her destiny with Aaron would eventually unfold in the current life.

She was also curious as to whether her past life connection with him was real or if it was a psychological fantasy. If the karmic link did exist, what then would be the eventual outcome of that connection? The two of them were intimate lovers in their past life and she had left him without fulfilling her promise. In the current life, the two of them had also been lovers, but he was the one who left her and through an empty promise. Was this her retribution, or was it part of an unfinished relationship tussle between the two?

Thursday, 23 December
⇨ *2:30 am*

Even though now I've forgiven Aaron but I guess or I should say I'm very definite that he'll not contact me. So let's just wait and see what will happen. People always say the future is a mystery. So let's wait and see the mystery then! Right now although I felt that I've the new found freedom and my life is so much more peaceful and happy, but there is still a little part of me can't find the total inner peace. Maybe it's because of Aaron? I have no idea ...

On Christmas Eve, Petrina took an afternoon nap and experienced another scary dream. She had flashes of images of herself back in her past life again. She vividly dreamed of herself as a Manchurian Empress dressed up in a Qing Dynasty court robe that was bright yellow with the phoenix embroidered on it. There was a lifelike quality about this dream that made a deep, lasting impression on her. I was quite

164

sure that it was a sign of her unconscious mind tapping into her past life.

She recalled vividly that the gown she was wearing had no waistline. She wore a jacket with horseshoe sleeves over the gown. On her head was a Manchurian court crown that was semi-conical in shape and sewn with red wefts. The crown was adorned with gold pheasant patterns, gems and jade. A yellow silk ribbon embellished with jewels could be seen hanging down from the back of the collar. The neckline of her dress was made of golden filament and decorated with pearls and jade ornaments. There were three sets of necklaces hung around her neck and over the front of her chest. In addition she wore a set of Manchurian shoes that required her to walk on high-platform soles.

Fig. 19: "Someone who looked exactly like me!"

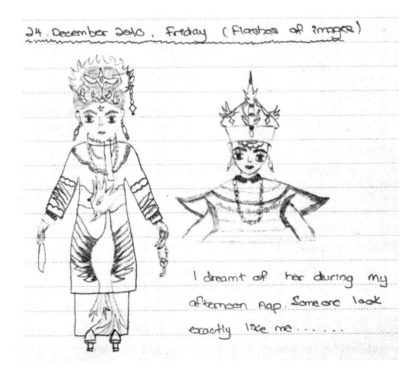

24 . December 2010 , Friday   (Flashes of image)

I dreamt of her during my afternoon nap. Someone look exactly like me . . . . . .

⇨ **Friday, 24 December** *(Flashes of images)*

I'm quite shocked to really see someone that looks like me dress in that way ... can't figure out why? Is she really my past life? I have never really studied history, so have no idea which dynasty the dressing belongs to ... But one thing I see in common is the key in her hand ... It's the one I've been drawing when I lost my memory. What is the link? What exactly does it mean? What's the story behind it? Have no idea ... the images are so clear that I could even see right in the middle of the heart shape is a red ruby (the key). Does this key really exist?

Upon waking she had the uneasy feeling that the dream was as real as her current life. She immediately got hold of her diary by her bedside and sketched the past life image of herself as the Empress. The level of detail that she could recall and reproduce was remarkable. The drawing represented a level of artistic skill that she had never been able to achieve in the past and it was amazing to her.

"I can't draw ... and I don't understand how I drew this out." Petrina was laughing away when she showed me the drawings of the Empress (Fig. 19) in her diary. When I looked at the drawings for the first time, I agreed with her that it was no easy feat to reproduce such fine details from a dream.

"When it comes to the dragon, I could never finish the drawing before. Never once could I finish the drawing like this ... never once," she kept emphasizing. "When I was in secondary school I was given a project to draw this kind of a sketch, and I could never finish it. Now I wonder how I could have drawn this out." She scrutinized her own artwork again in amazement.

I never had any doubt that these dreams experienced by Petrina were past life dreams. Such dreams were well known for their vividness. Through her regression therapy, she had already got herself on her path of increasing spiritual awareness and I believed that these dreams could be a harmonious way to work off her karma.

Generally speaking, karmic dreams are designed to bring unhealed past life issues to the forefront of our awareness. I therefore saw the past life dreaming as a good thing for her because she had eagerly wanted a change in the circumstances of her present life. I reflected over it. Perhaps for that to happen it would require healing of her past life blockages.

My understanding of past life integration is that it is an individuation process and is something that goes beyond a past life recall. An identification with a past life personality has an impact on our personal development and tends to obscure the blueprint of our current life. A successful integration with one's past life will not only be life-enriching but also opens the heart in compassion for others.

In Petrina's dream, she was holding the same key with the heart-shaped bow that she had previously drawn on several occasions. The images were so clear that she could visualize the key in her left hand, with a red ruby in the middle of the heart-shaped bow of the key. The dream and the images were so vivid that it stamped a memory on Petrina for the days and weeks that followed.

*****

Four days later the image of the past life Emperor were still sharp and clear in Petrina's mind. She decided she would reproduce them in her diary (Fig. 20). The Emperor was wearing the yellow dragon robe. He looked exactly like Aaron. The front of the robe was embroidered with one big dragon head. The rest of the dragon body with its fins and scales were twined round the robe. Likewise, the sleeves were horse-heel shaped. He wore a court crown with a round top edged with an upward brim. The jewel top had four tiers of pearls with one big oriental pearl being embedded on the top tier.

Fig. 20: "My past life husband, the Emperor, looks exactly like Aaron"

"My past life husband, the Emperor, looks exactly like Aaron," Petrina wrote in her diary after she had done the drawings. "Just can't help keep wondering if I am thinking too much or just some part of me is still unable to let go of the already eroded relationship ..."

What had not been resolved was the issue of the *key*. Did this key really exist in her past life or was it just a symbolic message? According to Petrina she could see vividly that the key was in gold and, apart from the ruby in the center of the bow, the key chain was made up of a string of pearls. What, if any, was the karmic link behind all these happenings?

Chapter Fourteen

The Key Link

When someone has a strong intuitive connection, Buddhism suggests that it's because of karma, some past connection.
– Richard Gere

For the first time, Petrina spent her Christmas and New Year's Day alone. It felt kind of weird for her. Even though Joshua and her weren't as close as when they just got married, they had been spending their Christmas Days together before they broke up. However, this year, the "home alone" feeling reminded her of her earlier feelings of emptiness (Fig. 8) and helplessness.

⇨ **Saturday, *25 December***
This year I'm all alone, still not quite used to it. Guess it's gonna take quite sometime to adapt to it. After all I believe no one wants to be alone ... Having a companion to talk to is always a good thing. Too bad for my case maybe the right one has not appeared yet, or he never existed. But on the other hand being alone I can say it's something good as you don't really have to bother to care about going out with anyone will cause your partner to feel upset. I can do whatever I want ... of course this comes with the lonely feeling ... I guess this is inevitable.

Petrina was due to return to work on Monday, 27 December after the Christmas holidays. Her experience of struggling through her illness in the past month was unforgettable. The process of retrieving her repressed memory while in depression was itself a major trauma. She had continued to consciously let go of her stored pain – the pain that was associated with her relationship with Aaron. She knew this was a way she had learned to forgive herself and others. Although forgiveness had released a lot of her emotional tension, she also found that after letting go, she began to experience difficulty trusting other people.

⇨ **Sunday, *26 December***

Now I look back its like I'm reading a story book. Though I've learned to look at things in a more positive way but still I guess as for Aaron the hope is too high which is why still there's some part that I still can't let go. Though the disappointment is there but I guess love is blind. No matter how much disappointment I have for Aaron I'm still able to forgive him. At least now I won't bother to question myself why he did that.

To me it's over and I'm moving on, that's the most important thing, I believe. If I can get over Joshua I can get over Aaron as well. Since the hurt is still there, what I can do now is lock my heart up until the wound heals. As time goes by Aaron will no longer affect me. Between Sadness and Happiness, I have chosen to be happy and let nature takes its place.

As each week passed by another layer of anxiety and fear was stripped away from Petrina as she went in search of her true self. At times she felt that something might be missing and that she had to search for answers. Yet, as she searched she found that she had to work through some of her fears, and that included her fear of abandonment.

On her first day back at work, she appeared much more tranquil and confident compared to the time before she was hospitalized. Many of her colleagues were astonished at her quick and dramatic recovery. Some of them were more drawn to her while others doubted her readiness to return to work. The HR Department had received my assurance that she was physically fit to return to work. Nonetheless they were cautious about delegating job duties to her. They changed her reporting structure. She was told henceforth to report directly to her manager instead of her former supervisor, Shirlene. This removed the previous environmental stressor from her. Then they limited her work responsibilities to handling patient registrations only and exempted her from the billings. While the intention was good, it made her bored.

Later in the day, she was asked to consider a change in her job scope. Two options were available – either as an administrative assistant doing data entry, filing and minutes writing, or work in an equivalent position attending to international patients at a private clinic. For a while Petrina was considering the second offer at the private clinic, because the job was associated with higher pay and allowed her time to further her studies in the evening.

Unlike her previous supervisor, the new manager she was reporting to was extremely nice and helpful. He surprised her by personally calling up various polyclinics to ask for possible job opportunities on her behalf. However, she now found herself experiencing increasing difficulty trusting another man.

On 30 December, Petrina had a third karmic dream. She dreamed about herself being in a dark room and heard someone asking: "Are you waiting for Aaron? The *key* is with him ..."

The very mention of the *key* disturbed her. She had been drawing the key in three previous pictures in her diary (Figs. 6, 7, 15) and twice as part of her karmic dreams (Figs. 9, 19). Until now she had no idea why and how she did it. The fact that she kept drawing it unconsciously suggested that she had a strong karmic link with Aaron to grapple with.

⇨ *Thursday, 30 December*

It's about the key again! Aaron has now become a ghost non-stop haunting me! No doubt I still feel for him but just can't figure out why is it so that after what he has done to me the bond towards him is still very strong ...

After experiencing past life dreams repeatedly, Petrina was a little overwhelmed by her curiosity over the destiny with Aaron. She decided to go for a divination in the Bugis Guanyin Temple at Waterloo Street. This temple was a favorite spot for augury and was always packed with tourists and local visitors. According to legend, wishes made in here often came true.

Upon entering the temple, she lit some joss sticks, prayed and asked a question quietly in her heart: "Is it over between the two of us? (herself and Aaron)

Next she took in her hands the container of "qian" or bamboo divination sticks. She shook the container until one bamboo stick with a lot number fell out. From the open shelves, she obtained a matching slip and interpretation sheet that contained a verse in Chinese characters. She took the slip to the resident soothsayer of the temple and asked for help in the interpretation.

"Unfinished business will be done," the soothsayer behind the table read the slip and paraphrased the interpretation for her.

Petrina was a little startled and didn't know what to say! What exactly was this unfinished business? And would the outcome be a positive one?

*****

Petrina arranged a further clinic appointment with me on 5 January 2011. We discussed her concerns and both felt the need to probe further into her past life issues. It was my intention to work with further past life regressions to comprehend the full complexity of the problem.

172

She turned up at 3:30 pm in her usual happy mood. She was again serene and radiant in her appearance. She was wearing her corporate uniform consisting of a flowery blouse, a turquoise jacket and a dark-blue skirt and black shoes. She greeted me warmly and we quickly got into an interesting dialogue.

She was frank and realistic about her recovery process. More importantly, her life perspectives had changed. "Of course I cannot improve overnight. It is not possible. Although the trust is dead between Aaron and I, but I still believe in keeping him as a friend whom I want to help ... in a way, as in letting him know that he was causing someone hurt, and so please don't do it again. So indirectly I am giving back to society."

I liked the way she looked at things positively. Although her progress had been remarkable, there were still a few ripples in her once turbulent pool. On the whole, it was a wonderful outcome. Unlike pharmacological effects, the hypnotherapy did not work by suppressing her symptoms. Rather it released her pent-up emotions through catharsis. All her major symptoms had vanished. We both felt proud of her achievement.

For this second past life session, I didn't need to use any lengthy induction. Her emotions were strongly focused on the image of the *key*, and I decided to use the emotions surrounding the *key* as the affect bridge. For this session I also intended to guide her to examine each supercharged thought, feeling and body sensation throughout the regression process.

"Close your eyes and take three deep breaths ... Focus your conscious awareness on the image of the key ... See if you can sense some emotions coming up."

Petrina rapidly went into a trance state.

"I am being protected ..." she whispered softly.

"Focus now on your feeling of protection and recall another time when you felt this same way. Let this feeling take you back to a past life when you were having the same feelings of protection."

"I am in a garden," she whispered again. "There are rivers ... and lots of soldiers around." She started describing.

"Look at yourself. What costume are you wearing?" I was trying to embody her in her past life.

"I see a phoenix on my costume."

"Who are you in this past life?"

"I am the Empress." There was no doubt that she was back in the same past life in the Qing Dynasty that she had experienced before.

"How old are you?"

"Twenty-six," she said after some hesitation.

"Look at your feet, and describe your footwear to me."

"It's very tight ..." She searched for words and then stopped.

"Are you wearing anything on your head?" I encouraged her to continue talking.

"Yes, a hat ... very heavy ... there are flowers ... in gold color."

"What color is your dress?"

"Red, black and golden."

"Is there anybody else next to you?"

"The maid. She is pouring tea. We are waiting ... the Emperor is coming back."

"Is he here already?" I asked after waiting a while.

"No."

"But you know he is coming?"

"Yeah ..." she paused and then continued. "The dead body of a white tiger ... It is a dead body sent by the Emperor."

I was surprised at the description. The white tiger is traditionally known to be a supernatural animal in China. It is known to preside over the western quadrant of the sky in Chinese metaphysics. It is a symbol of strength and power. I was wondering what was the relevance of the white tiger in her past life story.

"What else did you see?"

"The *key* is hanging around the body of the tiger." She continued to surprise me.

"Describe the key to me." I wanted to know if that was the same key that had been impacting her life.

"Gold color … with a red ruby in the center." It sounded identical to her earlier description.

"What did the soldiers say about the body of the dead tiger?"

"It's a gift from the Emperor." Then silence prevailed. I sensed that more things were happening than she could describe.

It turned out that Petrina was deeply engaged in visualizing an imperial ritual being carried out. The white tiger was lying on top of a very long white table covered with a yellow cloth. A number of gold plates were laid around the tiger. The plates were made in the form of lotus-shaped candle-holders. Nine candles were visibly burning away. Dates were engraved on the candles and written on the paintings that were hanging at the ceremony site. The dates were written in traditional Chinese characters which she couldn't figure out. However, in one of the candles, she saw a set of characters which she recognized to mean the eighth month (八月). A priest was praying at the ceremony. On the table were a bowl of wine and a basin of water with a knife placed next to it. In front of her on the table were two special wine cups, one with a carving of the dragon and the other with the carving of a phoenix. All these images were very clear and vivid.

"What happened next, after you have seen the key?"

"The Emperor's back."

"Describe the Emperor to me?"

"He is tall, very tanned … Oh! He looks exactly like Aaron!"

Apparently the ritual that was being carried out was intended to be a bonding ceremony and declaration of eternal love between the Emperor and herself as the new Empress. The Emperor took the knife, cut his finger with it and allowed his blood to drip from the wound into the bowl of wine which was then mixed with water. After that, he poured part of the content of the bowl onto the key and poured the balance into the two wine cups. Then she and the Emperor each took a wine cup and drank from them together as they declared eternal love for each other.

"I want you to ask the Emperor why is the key hung around the tiger's neck."

"He put it around the neck himself. It's a protection for me. He said that this is the key to our life. The key will protect me and I will be with him until he dies."

"What were your emotions when you heard that?"

"Touched."

"Any thoughts in your mind that goes with the emotion?"

"Guilty."

"What makes you feel guilty?"

"I killed the Empress."

"What happened next?"

"The Emperor took the key off the tiger's neck and asked the maid to wash it. Then he sent the key to me in a box. It's a wooden box."

I remembered she had previously drawn this wooden box twice in her diary (Figs. 6, 7) but without knowing the significance then.

"Tell me more about the box."

"There is a letter inside the box. It says that the key is a token of love. It is the key to his heart and my heart ... I accepted the key."

"After that what happened?"

There was a pause before the story continued.

"The Emperor came. He says he is tired. I helped him to the bed ... the Emperor is sleeping. I can't sleep. So I washed the Emperor's legs and feet. After that I fell asleep."

"Move to the point when you woke up and tell me what happened?"

"The Emperor sent a lot of doctors to me ... I am pregnant. They prescribed a lot of medicine."

"What stage is your pregnancy now?"

"Three months."

"What happened next?"

"I have nightmares because I killed the Empress."

"What happened next, after you experienced all the nightmares."

"I killed myself."

"Tell me how you killed yourself?"

"I hanged myself." Again, there was consistency with her previous regression.

"What is the stage of your pregnancy when you hanged yourself?"

"Three and a half months."

"Where are you now? Are you still in your body or have you left?"

"I have left."

"Have all the energies left your body?"

"Yes."

"Right, I want you to go all the way to the spirit realm and speak to your spirit guide ... Tell me, are you able to see the spirit guide now."

"Yes."

"Can you ask your spirit guide about the significance of the key?"

"He laughed ... The Emperor loves me."

"Can you ask him what is the connection between the key in this past life and the key in your present life?"

"It is a promise. I promised the Emperor that I would grow old with him together."

"I want you to meet the Emperor in the spirit realm now, at the count of three. One, two, three ... Is he there now?"

With techniques borrowed from psychodrama, I was trying to encourage her to dialogue with other characters from that lifetime, so that new understanding could be gained.

"Yes."

"Is there anything you want to say to the Emperor that you did not have a chance to say when you were alive?" I prompted the dialogue so that any apologies could be made at this time and guilt assuaged.

" I say sorry to him. He says that I will make up."

"Ask him how does he expect you to make up?"

"He will come to me."

"How will he come to you? And, when will he come to you again?"

"He didn't answer me."

"Is there anything else you want to say to the Emperor before you leave?"

"There will be more. I love him a lot."

"Has the Emperor anything to say to you before you depart?"

"He says he'll see me in my next life."

"Now, would you like to see the Empress you killed in the spirit realm?" I thought I would encourage her to resolve all her issues at this point.

"No," she blurted out.

"Can you ask the spirit guide for the last time; is there any pattern in this past life that is being repeated in the current life?"

"He says I am stubborn!"

After this I brought Petrina out of trance. The moment she emerged, she verified that Aaron was definitely the past life Emperor.

I had re-enacted the death point of her past life as far as the opportunity allowed because that was the psychological event with the most bearing on her wellbeing in her present life. In a horrible death like hanging, I would expect her to have died incomplete, without saying goodbye to her loved ones. All the negative emotions that she was preoccupied with at the moment of death, including guilt, fear and resentment, could have adhered to her soul and travelled intact into her current life. I thought her re-living the death point could have provided the opportunity to reverse much of the effects of the negativity. However, stubbornness stood in her way.

"Anyway, this past life session is about the *key* and its link. It is more like a pledge that I have actually made with the Emperor," she said after she emerged.

By now Petrina had obtained a clearer picture of what the karmic link was about and how it had been affecting her. The *key* had now pointed backwards to an origin in her past life. What was unspoken was that it would point forwards to potential future changes between herself and Aaron.

"With this pledge, I can understand the affinity between us. What worries me more is whether he will come back to haunt me later on!" She laughed. I thought her concern was legitimate.

Petrina was able to talk freely about Aaron at this stage. "He is the most terrible man I have ever met," she giggled. "In fact he is even worse than Joshua. At least Joshua has the guts and owns up for what he has done, but Aaron has done everything and pushes all responsibilities away." She laughed again.

"Anyway, it is over …" she continued meekly. "Such a grown-up man and doesn't even dare to answer for what he has done!" She said it calmly with absolutely no signs of agitation. I would have expected her willingness to forgive Aaron would signal the end of the unfinished business. But although the relationship had ended, the love may not have died.

She left the clinic that afternoon and seemed to have enjoyed the past life therapy session tremendously.

Chapter Fifteen

The Transformation

If you want to shrink something,
You must first allow it to expand.
If you want to get rid of something,
You must first allow it to flourish.
If you want to take something,
You must first allow it to be given.
This is called the subtle perception
Of the way things are.

— Tao Te Ching

P etrina's distressing symptoms had completely disappeared now. It was increasingly obvious to all her colleagues and friends that she had progressed beyond the initial stage of recovery. The change in her persona had struck everyone as being very sudden, rapid and astonishing.

She had stopped having past life dreams since the last regression. Furthermore, she had not been experiencing spontaneous visions of the image of the key. Everything seemed to point to the conclusion that her karmic ties with Aaron had faded to the extent that it no longer bothered her at the unconscious level.

She was now consistently radiant in her complexion and magnetic in her social interaction with others. Her work colleagues were increasingly drawn towards her at work. Even the elderly health attendants in the Ophthalmic Clinic would warmly invite her to join them in their smoking session and chitchat during the lunch hour. On her part she would freely mingle with them without any qualms.

Her past image was that of a shy and introverted little girl who kept things largely to herself. After her discharge from hospital, her personality had never been the same. In the past when someone was rude to her she would respond with anger, and when things didn't go her way she would become frustrated very quickly. Her outspoken attitude and extroverted tendencies now seemed to have enabled her to handle difficult customers at the front-line counter quite seamlessly these days.

In the past, Petrina was very conscious of her lack of security. She once talked to me about Maslow's Hierarchy of Needs and described how she had been stuck at the "security" layer of the hierarchy at one point in time. She had been asking herself how would she ever be able to bring security to her family? Then she got the wrong idea of marrying early as a solution. She thought by getting married she would be able to get someone to give her the security she needed. She laughed as she recapitulated how she managed her earlier life.

Now she saw things differently. She admitted that her early marriage was a mistake. What she looked for in the marriage was security and she paid a dear price to learn that it was never there. Paradoxically, now that she was divorced, she felt very secure. She could give happiness to herself now. She never had the chance of experiencing security and happiness in the past, but now she had them both.

"Being around with a family is a blessing," she said cheerfully. "A lot of people don't have family around them ... Still the same old words – be content with what you have and you will be happy.'

Cautiously, I brought up the subject of her feelings for Aaron again. I wanted to be sure that she no longer harbored any residual, negative feelings for that man.

"No. Not at all. Why would I want to continue the karma?" she said phlegmatically. "It is a cycle, and I see the cycle going round. If I don't start by being the one who breaks the cycle, then maybe my children in future ..." she paused with a subtle sadness in her voice. "I might have or might not have children in future, because my gynecologist said that I aborted too often, but they might suffer if the karma continues."

I was impressed. Her thinking was enlightened. It was obvious that she had already made her journey out of depression and was feeling a connection with something that had touched and transformed her life. I remembered when I first met her in the wards on 24 November, she was guilt-stricken. Now she was able to use forgiveness as the antidote to her guilt that had darkened her view of the world. She was now able to open herself to others whom she had, at one stage, rejected. I felt I had a lot to learn from her.

Petrina visited me again in my clinic on 13 January. She maintained her clinical improvement and her inner peace was shining brightly. She had severed all her connections with Aaron. I sensed that we were soon approaching a termination point in her therapy. By now she had been able to put all her past emotional insults and handicaps behind her. However, I wanted to deliver an additional session to minimize the chances of her repeating her failures in future. Moreover, a repeat regression to the same past life would uncover details missed out in earlier sessions and would reinforce the inner healing.

She sank quickly into a trance state as I used a hypnotic induction method. Bringing her back to the same past life was a straightforward task. Her body posture relaxed quickly as her long black hair was spilling over the pillow in rivulets.

Petrina regressed back to a time in China when she was the Empress during the Qing Dynasty. Again, she could identify the Emperor very clearly as Aaron. The same key that kept appearing in her dreams and her drawings was hanging round his neck.

"I am with the Emperor in a court session," she whispered.

"What is being discussed?" I asked.

"There is a drought. The Emperor is sending people to the place to help them."

"What is your role in it?" I questioned.

"I help the person in charge to prepare and send rations to the victims. Also ... sending doctors to help them."

Later I gathered from Petrina that the Emperor took the key off his neck and placed it around hers before they left together for the trip.

"What happened next?"

"I follow the Emperor to the town. He wants to see how people lead their lives ..."

"There is a crowd of beggars and I feel sorry for them," she continued. "The Emperor gives orders for houses to be built for them. The weather is too hot ... I fainted ... We go back to the inn ... and the doctors come ..."

"What did the doctors say about your fainting?"

"I am pregnant ... five weeks ... We go back to the palace. The Emperor brings a lot of gifts."

"What are your emotions at that time when you know you are pregnant?"

"Lost ... "

"What did you do next?"

"Rest ... I am taking a lot of tonics ... I feel nauseated ... the Emperor is happy. He visits me every day. The people in the palace are preparing for the baby to come ... I am two months pregnant now ... I am not happy. I am not ready to be a mum."

"What happened when you find that you are not ready?"

"I keep it to myself ... I go into depression ... I dream of the previous Empress and I feel guilty. This goes on for one month, and at the end of it I commit suicide ... I don't deserve to be happy, because I killed the Empress."

She had gone to her death point by then and all her energies had left her body. I brought her to the spirit realm to meet up with her spirit guide to find out the lesson she was supposed to learn from this lifetime.

"Move on," she said.

"Ask your spirit guide if there is a pattern in the past life that is being repeated in your present life."

"Stubborn."

"Meet up with the past Empress in the spirit realm. Is she there now?"

"Yes."

"Do you recognize her as someone you know in the present life?" I asked carefully, hoping to pick up an important clue.

"No," she replied firmly.

"Speak to her and say whatever you did not have a chance to say when you were alive."

There was silence.

"Is there anything she wants to say to you?"

"It's retribution ..."

"What does she mean by retribution?"

"Aaron."

"What does she mean by that?" I felt intrigued.

"Don't know ..."

"Anything else you want to say to her?"

"No," she said stubbornly.

"How do you feel towards her now?"

"I don't owe her anything," she retorted.

"Does the Emperor have anything to say to you?"

"He says it is not ended yet."

"Ask him what does he mean by that."

"He says: 'If I cannot have you in this life, you are still mine in the next life.'"

"How did you reply to him when you heard this?"

"Nonsense!" There was a tone of defiance in her voice.

"Now ... is there anything else you want to say to him before you leave?"

"No."

"I would like you to meet up with your unborn baby at the count of three. Do you see the baby now?"

"Yes."

"Do you have anything to say to him?"

"Sorry ..."

"Would you like to give him a hug before you leave him?"

"No."

"Don't you feel sorry for him?"

"Yes."

"Don't you want to give him a hug?"

"No. I don't want to."

"At the count of three I will ask you to leave the spirit realm and go to a place of healing." After that I left Petrina to immerse herself in the healing energy of the environment for several moments before eventually bringing her out of trance.

She emerged peacefully. She looked calm and composed and gave a smile soon after opening her eyes. After she got up from the couch, she concluded that her karmic link with Aaron was not entirely over. However, I had a feeling that whatever might happen next would be unlikely to result in reconciliation or upset her to any significant extent.

In the days that followed, Petrina's life returned to normal. She updated me at less frequent intervals now. She had gone back to her social groups and was experiencing much fun with them after work. She had also re-opened her Facebook account so that she could pursue her social networking more actively.

On 27 January, I received a sudden, emotional message from Petrina. She had made a startling discovery for herself through Facebook surfing. She visited Aaron's Facebook page and discovered something that shocked her!

Apparently Aaron had been having a close relationship with a girl called Cordelia and they had been going steady since 25 December 2009. Cordelia worked at a bank and her relationship with Aaron had started some seven months before Aaron and Petrina started dating each other.

This was another moment of truth, but an emotional one!

Petrina had initial difficulty grappling with the hurt that had resulted. She had always hated lies, and the feeling of being lied to was worse when the dishonesty involved romantic relationships. Aaron had already broken a promise to her once before and hurt her badly in the process. With this new finding it immediately raised several questions: Was Aaron ever serious with their relationship in the past? Did his parents really object to their relationship in the first place? And if they did, was that the pivotal reason for the breakup? Or was it because all along he never wanted to abandon Cordelia?

There was no way for her to obtain the answers. She next visited Cordelia's Facebook page to find out more. As her profile picture appeared on the computer screen, she felt a sense of uneasiness and something haunting about the photo – the thin eyebrows, flat nasal bridge, sharp chin and the soulful countenance. As she stared at the profile picture and allowed herself to sink deeper into her appearance, a bolt of familiarity surged through her entire body. She felt she must meet up with this lady!

She arranged to meet Cordelia in person and could hardly believe the truth when they stood face to face with each other. It was a staggering recognition – Cordelia was the Empress whom she had met in her past life while she was an imperial concubine! This sudden familiarity jolted her from head to toe and she took a minute to absorb this realization.

The pieces of the karmic puzzle had finally arrived and fitted themselves perfectly together. This lady whom she hated so much in her past life was back. Aaron and his past life Empress had come back to haunt her in her present life! It was an emotional moment and an unnerving shock! Her past life story was being replayed in her current life, but with a modified script. It was heartbreaking.

Over the next two days, she reflected over the situation. Then she asked herself several times: Why shouldn't I accept what has happened? Why can't I use forgiveness as the antidote to what had once darkened my life? Why should I define myself by who is against me?

Gradually she came to terms with the situation.

Saturday, 29 January
⇨ *12:13 pm*
If Aaron can betray me once, he can do it again to her ... As Aaron and I have too much drama going on in the past already, so even though they are together I believe he will still remember that he owes me a lot and this will remain deep in his heart. Ultimately Cordelia will feel the pressure ... I feel sorry for her, like how I feel in my past life.

The past life regressions had been self-validating for Petrina, but more importantly they provided significant healing. Her heart was so much more gracious than before. However, the experience of feeling the unfinished business being carried over from one life to another had intensified after she met Cordelia. This had been quite overwhelming.

After some time, another wave of realization struck her. If she had killed this lady in her past life and she was now back in the current life and entangled in the same romance triangle, was she destined to repeat the same pattern? And if she was destined to repeat a past life pattern now, was there a way to change the karmic cycle?

Saturday, 29 January
⇨ *7:38 am,*
I feel the emotion as really strong ... It's pretty hard to tell what exactly happened between the three of us but it's kind of a shock that everything is repeating exactly what happened during the past life.

I was concerned that Petrina's illness symptoms could be re-precipitated with this new turn of events. However, it did not happen. As in any path of personal evolution, she had to face obstacles, dangers and difficulties, but this fact had not deterred her from proceeding with her way of natural enfoldment. Her strong self-awareness had saved the day. She understood that the ultimate choice of whether she wanted to actualize or betray her potentialities stayed with her.

Days passed. She did not experience any further blackouts nor hear any of the voices that used to haunt her. Calmness had stayed with her and her rationality prevailed. Her acceptance of reality was the "welcome" that she had extended to her self-awareness. It did not take long for her to decide that it was her free will that she could just sever her psychic cord with Aaron. She wanted to move on in life without looking back.

"You can rest assured that I am okay," she wrote to me cheerfully. "People always say time will heal everything, right? Nothing is impossible so long as I have made up my mind to move on ... Aaron is out of my future life totally ..."

*****

In the interim the HR department had not managed to arrange a suitable new position for Petrina. Nor was she keen to allow herself to stagnate in her current job. She wanted to further her education and was keen to move to a new job environment that would provide her with study time in the evenings.

Petrina actively searched out for job opportunities in the private sector. Eventually, after several interviews, she secured a job with a higher salary as a clinic assistant in a gynecology clinic in Orchard Road. Her last working day was 14 February 2011, and she happily informed me about it.

"Why a gynecology clinic?" I asked. With her history of three emotionally disturbing abortions, I was concerned with the risk of her negative emotions being triggered again.

"No worries," she replied. "I am prepared to face and accept my past; that is why I have chosen to work in a gynecology clinic ... I am still doing meditation every day. So no stress or unstable feeling at all."

Epilogue

Three months have passed since Petrina embarked on her transformational journey (Fig. 21). She is now re-living her life as a changed person in a different style. She has lots of fun in the evenings with her social group and tends to come home late at night.

Fig. 21: The Transformational Journey

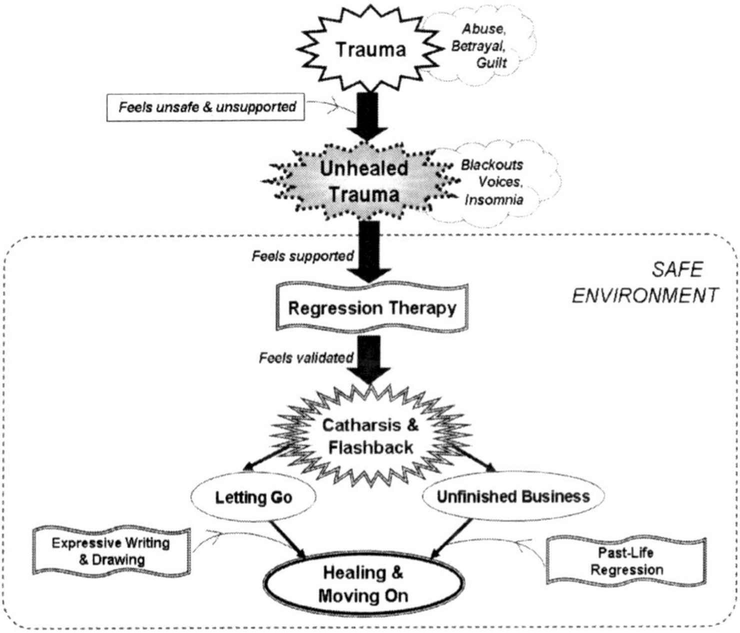

She is very happy with her new job as a clinic assistant and has since attained harmony with herself. Her boss at her new workplace is extremely friendly and caring to all his clinic staff and has delegated her to look after the clinic accounts and all financial matters. She gets along very well with her two other colleagues and enjoys the happy and pleasant work environment.

I feel wonderful one day when she encourages me to put the story of her illness and recovery in writing. She has found meaning and purpose in her life. She has also completed her unfinished business and put a closure to it. However, she has not forgotten Fabian.

13 March 2011 is Fabian's 28th birthday but unfortunately he is no longer around physically to celebrate. Petrina feels very sad on that day. Originally they had a joint holiday planned. She was to go on a short holiday trip with Fabian to celebrate his birthday and she has not forgotten it since. On that day, she feels extremely upset. There is an overwhelming sense of guilt on her part and she has problems finding inner peace.

She cries aloud at home that day. After releasing the emotions she feels better and dedicates a passage to him.

13th March, Happy Birthday to my dear friend who passed away last year ... I have lots of things to tell you ... Fabian. Happy Birthday! Regretfully I have been unable to make up for my past wrongdoing ... and my heart has been aching ever since ... Too many unhappy things have happened, including the irreparable mistake that I made. My hope now is that you are able to perceive my remorse from Heaven ... Henceforth I will treasure myself and my own life even more, so as not to disappoint you.

With this special message from her, she has put a closure to the lingering guilt that had been troubling her.

Appendix

In reading the story of a patient with roller-coaster emotions and myriad disturbing clinical symptoms, there is often a tendency to get absorbed in the details and lose sight of the big picture.

The graph below aims to plot the sequence of the different symptoms and events on a simple time line to show the clinical progress of Petrina during the relatively short period when intensive therapy was given. Of note is the abruptness with which her clinical symptoms came to a halt. What persisted during her recovery phase, however, were her karmic dreams. These strongly indicate a past-life connection as the basis of her current life issues.

Fig. 22: Clinical Progress Chart

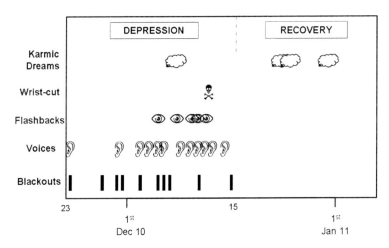

Glossary

Affect Bridge – a commonly used technique in regression therapy. The technique forms a bridge between affects and is used when the therapist attempts to locate the root cause of the patient's problem. When the patient presents his problem in the form of an emotion or a feeling, the therapist induces the patient into trance and gets the patient's subconscious mind to go back to the point in time when the emotion was first experienced. This effects regression back to the initial event that precipitated the problem.

Alprazolam – is a short-acting potent drug of the benzodiazepine class, often marketed as Xanax. It is used to treat moderate to severe anxiety disorders and panic attacks.

Amnesia – is the loss of a large block of inter-related memories.

Auditory hallucination – refers to the hearing of voices that have no physical source. The word "hallucination" comes from Latin and means "to wander mentally". Although the symptom is most commonly associated with schizophrenia and bipolar disorders, what is currently understood as its physiological basis is a failure to activate those areas of the brain associated with the monitoring of inner speech. The mechanism is one of confusion between "heard" speech and "inner" speech. When the distinction between speech and speech perception breaks down, the subject's own inner voice appears foreign. The utterance then takes on the quality of an alien voice or a voice speaking through the speaker.

Catalepsy – means strength, rigidity and immobility. It refers to the stiffening of the body or a specific body part, such as a limb, which can be induced by hypnotism. It is a characteristic of the trance state.

Catharsis – is a term often used in psychotherapy to indicate an extreme state of emotional release. The word originated from Greek and means "cleansing" or "purging". Aristotle used the term to describe the emotions experienced by the characters of a play or wrought upon the audience who watches a tragedy. The cleansing experience so derived was believed to have a corrective or healing effect. In hypnosis and regression therapy this term is used to describe the experiencing of the deep emotions associated with the events of the patient's past which had been inadequately addressed.

Chemotherapy – refers to the use of antineoplastic drugs for the treatment of cancer cells. It also refers to the combination of cytotoxic drugs used in an anti-cancer treatment regimen.

Clairvoyant – The term comes from French with *clair* meaning clear and *voyance* meaning vision. The word refers to someone who has the power of seeing objects or actions or gaining information beyond the range of natural vision.

CT Scan – is a specialized imaging technique that can produce cross-sectional images of the brain. It employs tomography created by computer processing. CT scanning of the brain is typically used to detect tumors, brain infarcts, trauma, hemorrhage and calcifications.

Demeter – is the Greek goddess of harvest, who controlled the seasons and presided over the sanctity of marriage. The story was that her daughter was abducted by Hades, god of the underworld. Life came to a standstill as the depressed Demeter wandered the Earth, searching day and night for her lost daughter.

Denial – is a complex defense mechanism that involves the individual's non-recognition of a problem so as to avoid his awareness of the reality of a traumatic experience. When this interferes with rational action to heal the hurt, it becomes a form of maladaption.

Dissociation – is a term coined by a neurologist, Pierre Janet, who first articulated the clinical principle of traumatic memories as the underlying cause of dissociative disorders. He described amnesia as being the cardinal feature of dissociation and explained how unintegrated, emotionally charged traumatic experiences leading to dissociation can influence one's inner life and relationships. These memories are usually accessible under hypnosis.

Divination – comes from the Latin word *divinare*, which means "to foresee". It is an attempt to gain insight to hidden knowledge or obtain an answer to a question by way of a ritual.

EEG – is the short form for electroencephalogram. It is a map of the spontaneous electrical activity of the brain recorded by putting multiple electrodes over the scalp.

Flashback – is an involuntary recurrent memory in which an individual experiences a sudden, powerful past experience. It is usually a personal experience that pops into one's awareness without any premeditated attempt to search. The memory is often a traumatic one.

Hero's journey – This is an archetypal concept that describes the trials and tribulations of an individual who experienced severe hardship to reap the fruits of his labor. The concept is derived from comparative mythology in which the "hero" in the ordinary world starts his journey to enter an unusual world of strange events upon receiving a call. After embarking on the journey he handles challenging tasks and solves difficult problems, often alone. At the peak suspense, the hero survives a severe challenge with help earned along the way. He then acquires a gift that helps him to discover important self-knowledge and to improve the world upon his return.

Hypnagogic – The hypnagogic state is the boundary zone between being awake and falling asleep. For some people this is a time when visual and auditory hallucinations occur.

Hypnosis – is a cooperative interaction in which the patient responds to the suggestions of the therapist. Its use was promoted by Dr. Elliotson, the physician who introduced the stethoscope to England. The term hypnosis is derived from *neuro-hypnotism* (nervous sleep) coined by the Scottish surgeon James Braid around 1841. Braid thought that it was hypnotic suggestion that was the basis of the healing. During World War I, when a tremendous incidence of shell shock was encountered, Ernst Simmel, a German psychoanalyst, used hypnosis for the treatment of war neurosis. The merger of hypnosis with psychoanalysis allowed hypnosis to play a prominent part in the treatment of combat fatigue during World War II. After World War II Dr. Milton Erickson clarified that hypnosis was really a state of focused concentration of the relaxed mind that we all entered into spontaneously and frequently.

Inner Child – is a concept in analytic psychology that refers to the childlike aspect of a person's inner psyche. It is that part of us which is alive, energetic, creative and fulfilled. It can also be considered as a subpersonality. Often the term refers to the emotional memory and experiences stored in the subconscious mind and used to address subjective childhood experiences.

Insomnia – refers to the difficulties of an individual in falling and staying asleep.

Karma – means "action" or "doing" and is used specifically for those actions that spring from the intention of someone who is not enlightened. Karma is the law of moral causation. It explains the cause of the inequality that exists among mankind. The inequality is attributed to not only heredity and environment but also to the results of our own past actions and our present doings. It reminds us that we ourselves are responsible for our own happiness and misery.

Lot – refers to a set of divination bamboo sticks thrown from a container to decide on the answer to a question by chance. The single bamboo stick with the corresponding LOT number will indicate the answer to the question.

Maslow's Hierarchy – is a motivational model developed by Abraham Maslow in the 1950 s. All of us are motivated by needs and Maslow explains how these needs motivate all of us. He argued that only when the lower-order needs of physical and emotional wellbeing are satisfied are we bothered with the higher-order needs of influence and personal development.

Meditation – refers to the practice in which an individual self-induces a mode of consciousness in order to attain inner peace and calmness. The word *meditate* comes from the Latin root *meditatum*, which means to ponder. In the meditative state, the individual experiences relaxation, concentration and an altered state of awareness. It corresponds to the alpha state of EEG recordings.

Mind's eye – refers to the natural human ability to experience visual mental imagery. Medically, the lateral geniculate nucleus and the visual cortex are known to be activated in fMRI studies during mental imagery tasks.

Nordazepam – is a benzodiazepine derivative and an active metabolite of diazepam and marketed as Nordaz. It has anxiolytic, muscle relaxant and sedative properties and is used primarily in the treatment of anxiety.

Parts therapy – is one of the techniques used in hypnotherapy for conflict resolution. It is founded on the concept that the individual's personality is composed of a number of different subpersonalities, or "parts". These different subcategories of personality each play a different role in the inner mind. In a deep hypnotic state, the therapist can speak to each of these "parts" and the patient can resolve his inner conflict upon emerging.

Past life dream – is usually very vivid in nature. Unlike ordinary dreams, past life dreams have a lot of historical detail, can seem like recurring nightmares and the individual is not able to change the sequence of events no matter how hard he tries. These dreams often explain strange habits and unusual behaviors and show the origins of the individual's emotional and spiritual issues.

Past life regression – is a technique used to recover memories of past lives undertaken in a psychotherapeutic setting. It involves the patient answering a series of questions while under trance to reveal his identity and events in a past life. The re-living of a past life and reframing of the experience of the events in the past life often helps in healing.

Pharmacotherapy – is the treatment of diseases and disorders through the use of drugs.

Psychotherapy – is the treatment of a psychological maladjustment by a range of psychological techniques such as psychoanalysis, group therapy or behavioral therapy.

Regression – the word means going back to an earlier or less advanced state. In the psychoanalytic context, it refers to the return of a chronologically earlier state or less adapted pattern of behavior. Regression therapy is a healing technique that is based on the premise that everything the individual has experienced contains a certain amount of emotion that is recorded in the subconscious mind.

Reiki – the word is made up of two Japanese words: "Rei" which means Higher Wisdom and "Ki" which is Life Force Energy. It is a healing technique administered by the laying on of hands to activate the natural healing processes of the patient's body. It is based on the concept that an unseen life force from the Universe flows through the Crown Chakra of the healer and is transmitted through the palmar surface of the healer's hands to the patient. It is an ancient Tibetan Buddhist technique of healing that was rediscovered by Dr. Mikao Usui in 1922 and redeveloped for widespread use.

Somnambulism – is a deep hypnotic state in which the patient has full possession of his senses but no subsequent recollection.

Sympathetic skin response test – is a simple non-invasive test to assess the integrity of the sympathetic nervous system. It involves the measurement of the electrical potential generated in sweat glands.

Therapy – comes from the Greek word *therapeia*, which means healing. In the medical context it refers to the treatment of a disease. When the term is used unqualified, it is often taken to be synonymous with psychotherapy.

Tilt table test – is a medical procedure used to find the cause of syncope. It involves having the patient lie flat on a special table while connected to ECG and blood pressure monitors. The table then creates a change in posture from lying to standing.

Tinnitus – is the perception of sound within the ear in the absence of external noise. The symptom is often described by the patient as a "ringing sound".

Vasovagal syncope – is a mode of fainting that is mediated by the vagus nerve of the brain. There is either (i) a drop in the heart rate leading to a reduced cardiac output or (ii) peripheral vasodilatation followed by a drop in the blood pressure leading to fainting.

Further Reading

Churchill, R., *Regression Hypnotherapy – Transcripts of Transformation,* **Transforming Press, 2002.** This book contains teaching material and full transcripts of current life regression sessions for a variety of conditions including phobias, grief, lack of confidence, sabotaging success, unhealthy relationships, abuse and fear of abandonment. It is an excellent guide for beginners and also a useful text for experienced therapists.

Engel, B., *The Emotionally Abused Woman – Overcoming Destructive Patterns and Reclaiming Yourself,* **Fawcett Books, 1992.** A psychotherapist who writes from her personal emotional scars has penned a wonderful book on understanding destructive patterns of the emotional abuser as well as the emotionally abused and on how to break the cycle to achieve healing.

Gordon, J.S., *Unstuck – Your Guide to the Seven-Stage Journey out of Depression,* **Penguin Books, 2008.** An internationally renowned psychiatrist and a pioneer in integrative medicine expounds his views on the use of drugs in modern biological psychiatry and how he uses an alternative method of helping his patients out of depression with a non-pharmacological approach.

LaBay, M.L., *Past Life Regression – A Guide for Practitioners,* **Trafford Publishing, 2004.** A light reading book on the practice of past life therapy that incorporates stories from the author's personal and professional experience. The author blends hypnotherapy techniques with philosophy, intuition and past lives to catalyze growth and transformation in her patients.

Lucas, W.B., *Regression Therapy – A Handbook for Professionals.* ***Vols. I & II,*** **Book Solid Press, 1992.** The two are a classic. It is a multi-author work on regression therapy compiled by a professional psychologist and Jungian analyst. Volume I focuses on past life therapy while Volume II touches on prenatal and birth experiences, childhood traumas and death.

Schwartz, R., *Your Soul's Plan,* **Frog Books, 2007.** An excellent in-depth exploration of why we incarnate, choose our parents and our life lessons using ten captivating case studies.

Ten Dam, H., *Deep Healing,* **Tasso, 1996.** Regression Therapy techniques used by Hans, who is one of the pioneers in Regression Therapy. Hans has trained students in Holland, Brazil and internationally for over 20 years.

Tomlinson, A., *Healing the Eternal Soul,* **O Books, 2006.** This is a definitive reference work in regression therapy. Andy shares his valuable experience in detail and uses concrete case studies to illustrate his points and techniques. This book is a must-have for any regression therapy practitioner and will captivate any reader interested in the subject.

Tomlinson, A., *Exploring the Eternal Soul,* **O Books, 2007.** Andy takes the reader beyond the death experiences and gives a wide and comprehensive explanation about Life-Between-Life regression therapy. He puts the content into a structured way that is easy to follow and understand what's happening. This is a highly recommended book to understand about our life choices, and also for readers who are curious about what lies beyond death.

Tomlinson, A. (ed), *Transforming the Eternal Soul*, **From the Heart Press, 2011.** Written as a follow-on from *Healing the Eternal Soul*, it's packed with illuminating case studies and specialized regression therapy techniques. The chapters include: empowering a client; working with difficult clients; spiritual inner child regression; clearing dark energy; crystal therapy in regression; and integrating therapy into a client's current life.

Whitfield, C.L., *Memory and Abuse – Remembering and Healing the Effects of Trauma*, **Health Communications Inc., 1995.** The author is a well-known psychotherapist and pioneer in helping people in distress from family violence and trauma. He shares his knowledge and experience with those in the helping profession who need to help their patients to heal.

Whitfield, C.L., *Healing the Child Within*, **Health Communications Inc., 2006.** This is one of the first books to explore and define the concept and principles underlying treatment of the "Inner Child" based on the author's observations of the healing process in those of his patients who had been traumatized as children.

Woolger, R.J., *Other Lives, Other Selves – A Jungian Psychotherapist Discovers Past Lives*, **Bantam Books, 1988.** A fascinating book that presents original insights into the emerging psychology of reincarnation. The book draws on both Western science and Eastern spirituality and explains how past lives may form the basis of transformation and healing our lives.

Woolger, R.J., *Healing Your Past Lives*, **Sounds True Inc., 2004.** This short book provides a series of interesting case studies that illustrates the power of uncovering past lives in the healing process. It gives insight as to how current life symptoms could be related to past life dramas and frozen memories. It also provides the reader with the key to unlocking the mysteries and questions they struggle with in their current lives.

Worthington Jr., E.L., *Forgiving and Reconciling – Bridges to Wholeness and Hope*, InterVarsity Press, 2003. A psychologist and counselor has written a wonderful book on the characteristics of forgiveness and the practical steps towards achieving both forgiveness and reconciliation. The wisdom of the book comes from both scientific research and the murder of the author's own mother.

Regression Therapy Associations

International Board of Regression Therapy (IBRT) – This is an independent examining and certifying board for past life therapists, researchers and training programs. Its mission is to set professional standards for regression therapists and organizations. The website has a list of international accredited past life training organizations.
Website: http://www.ibrt.org

Spiritual Regression Therapy Association (SRTA) – This is an international association of regression therapists that respect the spiritual nature of their clients. Established by Andy Tomlinson, they are professionally trained by the *Past Life Regression Academy* to international standards and work to a code of ethics that respects the clients' welfare.
Website: http://www.spiritual-regression-therapy-association.com

European Association of Regression Therapy (EARTh) – This is an independent worldwide association with the objective to create and maintain an international standard in regression therapy and improve and enlarge its professional acceptance. Every summer it offers a series of workshops for ongoing professional development. The website has a list of international accredited regression therapy training organizations.
Website: http://www.earth-association.org

About the Author

Dr. Peter Mack received his undergraduate medical education from the University of Singapore and undertook postgraduate specialization in the field of general surgery. He obtained his Fellowships from the Royal College of Surgeons of Edinburgh and the College of Physicians and Surgeons of Glasgow, UK. He practices in Singapore General Hospital and has several other academic qualifications. He has a PhD in Medical Science from the University of Lund, Sweden, and three other Masters degrees, in Business Administration, Health Economics and Medical Education. Over the years in his medical practice, he has developed a special interest in Clinical Hypnotherapy and has obtained certification from the National Guild of Hypnotists (NGH), International Medical and Dental Hypnotherapy Association (IMDHA) and the International Association of Counselors and Therapists (IACT). He also holds a Diploma in Regression Therapy from the Past Life Regression Academy (PLRA).

To contact the author email: dr02162h@yahoo.com.sg

Lightning Source UK Ltd.
Milton Keynes UK
UKOW022140200112

185763UK00012B/7/P